FLORIDA CAM

Victor M. Knight

PELICAN PUBLISHING COMPANY
Gretna 1997

Library of Congress Cataloging-in-Publication Data

Knight, Victor M.
Florida scams / Victor Knight.
p. cm.
Includes bibliographical references.
ISBN 1-56554-190-1 (pb : alk. paper)
1. Fraud—Florida. 2. Swindlers and swindling—Florida.
3. Florida—Social conditions. I. Title.
HV6698.F6K65 1997
364.1'63'09759—dc20 96-33542
CIP

Manufactured in the United States of America
Published by Pelican Publishing Company, Inc.
1101 Monroe Street, Gretna, Louisiana 70053

FLORIDA CAM

This work is dedicated to the person who has served (for at least several years) as wife, mother-of-kids, grandma-of-even-more, homemaker, support group, critic, analyst, booster, audience, applause-machine, laugh-track, and I don't know what-all, but who is suddenly exposed in her true calling: to Patty, a gifted editor and proofreader. (I would have bet cash money that nobody could find that many typos.) (And I do not use too many parentheses and . . .s.)

Contents

Acknowledgments

Any work such as this must be, of necessity, the product of a team effort. I would be greatly remiss if I failed to recognize the wonderful contributions made by so many friends, associates, and helpers, all of which resulted in this finished product.

First, my heartfelt thanks goes to attorney Robert Rex, partner in the Boca Raton law firm of Dickenson, Murdoch, Rex & Sloan. I thank Bob for his story contributions, his counseling, and his eagle-eyed proofing of the material.

Then, in the story department, I must salute Damon Runyon, Samuel Goldwyn, Frank Mankiewicz, and everyone remotely connected with the Broadway production and the movie of *Guys and Dolls,* the consummate showbiz study of scams. Runyon originally created the story; Goldwyn produced the movie; and Mankiewicz put down the immortal "cider-in-the-ear" words for Marlon Brando to say to Frank Sinatra in the movie.

Further along in the story department, the contributions from my media friends form the next plank in the structure. From the *Sun-Sentinel* Newspapers, my thanks to expert business editor Jack Nease for his many outstanding columns; to editorial writer Jim Driscoll for his comments on the Passing Scam Parade; and to investigative editor Fred Schulte for his exhaustive work on telemarketing. It was this work that helped Fred create his outstanding book *Fleeced* (Prometheus, N.Y.), which he so generously shared with me. Thanks also for his work on the ostrich eggs and own your own phone booth stories. And to my fellow *St.*

Petersburg Times alumnus, editorial columnist/writer, Tom Kelly—thanks for the great stories.

In the Tampa Bay area, thanks to Matt Walsh for a long-ago feature in *Florida Trend* magazine on the ESM scandal, and in part, the Marvin Warner story.

And my appreciation goes to Ron Stevens, Executive Director of the West Palm Beach Better Business Bureau, for his help and direction.

Back to my media friends, from the Knight-Ridder newspaper *The News,* source and story help on all the incredible Boca Raton scams came from both Clem Winke and Roger Cooven. Thanks also to Wayne Ezell and to Chamber of Commerce leader Mike Arts for his commentary.

My thanks to writers Danielle Herubin, Lisa Baertlein, and old friend Elliott Kleinberg from the *Palm Beach Post,* along with Mindy Brockman and pilot Jeff Margolf, for assists on the Let's Pretend Airline story, and a special thanks to ace wordsmith, columnist John Grogan.

From *The Washington Post,* Albert Crenshaw brought to light again the facts on the "repeat victim phenomenon." And, as always, I owe a major debt to veteran newsman, columnist, and author Stuart McIver for his help with the Gulf American story and its Florida land scams; also to eminent Florida authors Hampton Dunn, Michael Gannon, and old friend Bernard McCormick.

The intrepid McCormick, publisher, columnist, and sage of Fort Lauderdale, steered me to sources on Prince Michael of Austria.

Many thanks to Joan Morris of the Florida State Photographic Archives, and to William Warren Rogers and Frank Stephenson for their great work on the Popham oyster empire story.

My thanks to Ms. Diana Henriques of *The New York Times* News Service for the great stories on Boca's bogus businesses, and to *The News* publishers and editors for carrying these stories. A special thanks goes to Kurt Eichenwald of

The New York Times for his incredible book *Serpent on the Rock* (HarperCollins, N.Y.), *the* pre-eminent work on the Pru-Bache scandals. My thanks to state Senator Jim Scott of Fort Lauderdale, along with all the folks at CBS's "60 Minutes," for their work exploring Florida's bankruptcy laws.

And, speaking of *The New York Times,* it was great to find one of Fred Allen's classic radio lines joyously resurrected by Russell Baker in one of his nationally syndicated columns. The line sent me speeding to my Fred Allen library. (Which is certainly one of the very finest in all Live Oak.) I'm always glad to find another Fred-Allen-ophile.

More kudos are due the entire crew at Taxwatch, Inc., the Tallahassee group, for their supply of backup documentation on hundreds of old and new Florida scams.

In the computer/Internet/cyberspace department, thanks to resident computer genius Glen Rovinelli and to Atlanta correspondent Bruce Brawner for their explanatory contributions.

All of the above eventually leads us to the outstanding people at the Associated Press and to the APN Director of Special Projects in New York, Norm Goldstein. I must especially thank Norm for his kind and generous help. Without the work of several generations of AP veterans creating newswire feeds and press and radio stories, this work would not have been possible.

Thanks to Vern Thornton of the Sleuthing Seniors, and to Hank Thompson, who invented his "Instant Teaching Machine" so long ago.

It perhaps would have been easier just to group everyone together alphabetically, because I'm sure I'm going to miss some very special person along the line. So please forgive me if your name happens to be momentarily lost to me and is among the missing.

The generosity, counseling, and help from all of the above—along with many others—are the ingredients that made this project come to life.

All the characters, including the grandaddies, are very, very real. All the situations are factual, whether from long, long ago scams, or near-present-day operations. All comments, attributes, transactions, facts, and figures are triply-checked, verified, and many times validated from multiple sources as well as from first-generation, firsthand research, quotes, interviews, and stories.

All materials so generously provided by my colleagues are carefully quoted from the source. *Their* statements are correct. Any errors or omissions are my own.

My special thanks go to my own personal favorite fellow: Neal Anthony, head of that Bamboozled Retirees Association of America that you'll hear about later. Wherever you are, Neal, my thanks to you for giving me the rule that said, Regret is to folks what mud is to hogs—only good for wallerin' in. Neal is also the perfect personification of that famous ancient rule developed by Julius Caesar, just before he opened Caesar's Palace in 55 B.C. (George Burns said he is the only guy who played Caesar's Palace when it was owned by Julius.)

The rule said, *Non illegitimi carborundum.*

(That's Don't let the bastards grind you down.)

It should have been one of Grandaddy's Rules.

FLORIDA CAM

Introduction

Grandaddy's Rules and How They Grew

You know, having grandaddies is like that old saw about having kids—it's hereditary. If your folks didn't have any, chances are you won't either. It's like Papa Johnson used to say, "We've got a lot of heredity. It runs in our family."

Now having grandfathers is one of the greatest privileges any kid could have. And when you have *two* grandfathers, and both of them are Real Certifiable Characters, it's almost more than a gen-u-wine F.D.K. (Florida Depression Kid) could ever hope for.

Now I never called my grandfathers Grandfather, or Grandaddy, or Grampaw. In many parts of the Old South in those days, your immediate father was always called Daddy and your grandparents were called Papa and Mama, along with their respective last names—to distinguish them from Daddy and Mother.

Both of my grandaddies—Papa Johnson and Papa Knight—had their own personal, private sets of rules by which they did their "bin-ness," conducted their personal lives, and managed to "gitalong" with other folks. These rules applied whether the other folks were bin-ness associates, friends, or family (kinfolk)—or whatever—because all these categories often tended to overlap quite a bit. I think it was down around Grandaddy's Rule #15 or so that said, You always do your bin-ness with your kinfolk.

I've decided that the present generation really *needs* Grandaddy's Rules to learn how to gitalong, and that *somebody* ought to dig them out, shine them up, and place them in some kind of a display case, so folks could get to them and use them.

So I dug them up and worked them into this book. And you know, the more I got involved in *Florida Scams,* the more I realized what a truly wondrous connection there was between our present-day, scam-riddled culture and virtually every one of those good old Grandaddy's Rules.

As my Papa Johnson would say, "They's gonna be good for you and hep you, too." That was his good advice for everybody, all the time, about any problem.

Now, Papa Johnson was what folks might call today a big businessman. His folks had come down to Marianna, Florida, from Alabama in the early 1800s.

By a little after the turn of the century, Papa Johnson had acquired a general store, the town mill, and some land that the mill-run flowed through. He eventually lost it all in the panic of, say, about 1919, 1920, or 1921. Pick a panic, any panic at all.

So you might say Papa Johnson had lots of opportunities to learn, develop, and polish, firsthand, his set of Grandaddy's Rules—and to put them into action.

Now my Papa Knight was probably even more involved with his rules than Papa Johnson was with his. Papa Knight's own daddy and grandaddy had left their Georgia roots to come to the Lake City, Florida, area, also back in the early 1800s. Back then it wasn't even called Lake City. The settlement's first name was Corinth.

Papa Knight was Corinth's first postmaster. Now just so you won't go thinking that was too big of a deal, the post office was a hole in a big board fence with a bell hanging on a nail. If the mail-rider came through, Papa Knight or the kids would run out and ring the bell on the fence and folks would come around.

Anyway, Papa Knight, the postmaster, was known by the local folks as the town politician. They said he was sure going someplace. They didn't rightly know where, but someplace. As a matter of fact, when a bunch of young Corinth buckos would go sporting back up around Valdosta, where the family had come from, they would call Papa Knight the Duke of Lowndes County.

Then young Papa Knight went off to serve in the Florida state legislature, beginning around the 1890s—living proof that once in a great while, an innocent man is sent to the legislature.

After that he went through a whole series of Good-Old-Boy-Pork-Barrel-Political-Appointee jobs as if he were Sherman going through Georgia. He eventually worked his way around to Marianna, where it seemed divinely preordained that he was to run into Papa Johnson.

From here on out, sweet little old Marianna was never to be the same.

You can just imagine these two Certifiable Characters: tall, gaunt, domineering, taciturn, work-driven Papa Johnson, trying to hold absolute sway over his eight kids, and short, round, smooth-talking, bubbly, affable Papa Knight with *his* eight kids.

Boy howdy. What a mess it was in old Marianna! It's little wonder that a whole bunch of Grandaddy's Rules would come out of this magic potion.

These rules are guaranteed to help you gitalong in the land of the scam (Florida, in case you hadn't caught on). And just think—you're getting these valuable rules for *nothing*—or almost nothing. (It was Grandaddy's Rule # 1 that said, Ain't nuthin' ever fer nuthin'.)

And when these two good old boys got together—Marion Sylvester Knight, the politician-sport, from his family's roots in Georgia and Bew-fort, and James Willys Johnson, the merchant, from his family's roots in Alabama—man, the fur began to fly!

Papa Knight always said that he and Papa Johnson together could have taught a hummingbird to sing the lyrics. He was the more stylishly articulate of the two; after all, he'd been in the state legislature, you know. This isn't an ordinary bo-hunk cracker boy you're dealing with.

I suppose I could just go right ahead and give you all of Grandaddy's Rules in a bunch, right off, but that wouldn't make much sense, now, would it? In the first place, you wouldn't be able to handle this load of wisdom in just one dose. No, sir! These rules are serious stuff! And they *will* be good for you and help you too.

That's why the rules are so pertinent to your travels through *Florida Scams,* coming up just ahead.

Yes, sir; these two good old grandaddies had a rule for just about everything you could ever come up with . . . including the smooth-talking jasper in the checkered suit selling everything from books on farming to tractor tires . . . or the drummer who just got off the train carrying a suitcase full of anvils. These rules were a major part of the way you learned to gitalong in the Old South—and they'll help you today, too. As Papa Johnson used to say, he didn't have to worry about which side his bread was buttered on; he planned to eat both sides.

The Old Cider-in-the-Ear Trick

There is a classic scene in Samuel Goldwyn's great movie *Guys and Dolls* that just about says it all. In the scene, Nathan Detroit (Frank Sinatra) is trying to snare Sky Masterson (Marlon Brando) into a sucker bet for $1,000 on whether Mindy's sells more strudel than cheesecake on a given day. Sinatra already has the information, having been secretly checking strudel and cheesecake sales over previous days.

It's a true sucker bet if ever there was one, but Brando is too hip to go for the scam. In one of the great short monologues in showbiz history, Brando replies in grand, Damon Runyonesque fashion, with words masterfully crafted by

Frank Mankiewicz that sum up every sucker bet, every con, every sting and set-up of all time.

In the monologue, Brando says something like, "When I left home, my daddy gave me some mighty wonderful advice. He said son, one of these days in your travels, a guy is going to show you a brand-new deck of cards on which the seal is not yet broken. Then this guy is going to offer to bet you that he can make the jack of spades jump out of this brand-new deck of cards and squirt cider in your ear. But son, you do not accept this bet. Because as sure as you stand there, you are going to wind up with an earful of cider."

It is probably the finest summation of the con ever to appear on the silver screen—or anywhere else, for that matter. And it matches up well with all of Grandaddy's Rules.

Now you've probably heard the fellow or gal on the phone with the five hundred ball-point pens that they can let go at the absolutely unbelievable price of only $1.14 apiece because they were drop-shipped to a nearby town and the freight consignee had moved away. Or maybe you've been approached by Prince Michael of Austria, who could get you an unbelievable deal on a low-mileage, slightly-used Bugatti or Alfa Romeo, only driven very slowly in parades by his daddy, King Bob the Freckled.

Or maybe you've had the old siding game brought to your front door when you lived up north, where the fellows were actually deciding whether they were going to give you the old furnace-inspection routine or the roofing checkup as you answered the door on a frosty Toledo mid-morning. Or maybe they'd get your screens cleaned. Or, if you really measured up as a prospect, maybe they would "shoot the moon" and go for an entire aluminum siding job on your house. They had them all. These guys were so good at what they did that the entire con industry became known in some areas as the siding game.

Maybe you checked in with one of those famous pyramid

scams such as the penny-stock sales campaign. That's the one where the phone operator salesguys were driving your little twenty-cent stock up to almost a buck in just a few days—or even hours—and you couldn't believe your good fortune at having answered the phone when the "investment counselor" called your number. (He may have actually been a machine, but what did you know.) That was the one where your "dividend" was being paid out of proceeds from the next guy's purchase.

Or maybe you believed the ostrich egg dude. Or maybe you even invested in Willie Popham's Oyster Empire. Who knows . . . maybe you bought yourself some *telephone booths!* Boy, were you lucky!

Maybe you bought into some giant oil and gas limited partnerships being purveyed by some smooth-talking jasper in a three-piece suit, a $60 shirt, and custom-made *eye*-talian shoes. Maybe this was when you found out that you really weren't too sure just what a limited partnership *was.* And that was when you temporarily forgot Grandaddy's Rule #1. (It may have slipped your mind. It was a very small rule.)

All scams are simply variations of a few universal themes which appeal to the baser parts of human nature. They all work well some of the time—or even most of the time. And they all bring us to Grandaddy's Rule #1. (It goes back to the gold-rush days, when the miners and the mine owners negotiated that fifty-fifty split: the owners got the gold mine and the workers got the shaft.)

The rule was so very simple. It went, There almost never ain't nuthin' fer nuthin'! . . . or words to that effect.

No matter what form the con takes, they're all based on one universal ingredient: *you. You* are the indispensable part of any con. Without you, there will be no purchase, no scam, no loss. So that's why I've written this book, for *you!* It should be kept on your immediate person at all times. Never leave home without it.

You're going to find all of Grandaddy's Rules to be

mighty helpful, because someday, somewhere, some smiling, congenial good old boy is going to sidle up to you and say that he has just found a paper sack! And it has five thousand dollars in it! *And,* he has decided to split it with you! Just imagine your good fortune!

But then he says that he thinks you both should put up some good faith money, let's say $500, or maybe $50, depending on the neighborhood, and whether you're wearing your fake Rolex or not. He says, "This way, we can share this incredible good fortune with one another." At this point, your wheels should start whirling as your mental computer sifts through your files to determine the specific Grandaddy's Rule that will apply in this case. Don't worry, there'll be one all right—probably several. But when all else fails, Grandaddy's Rule #1 will always do.

Anyway, so you give him your $500, and he has to go to the bathroom . . . be back in just a moment. In other words, he *leaves.* (Here is where you should start your Key Word List. "Leaving" is something that should be avoided at all costs.) Really! It happens about ten thousand times each year, in America alone. It's called the "pigeon drop."

Yes, it'll happen—mark my words. It may not be in this exact setting or sequence; it may be for your life savings, or for just a ten-spot . . . but it'll happen. As sure as you stand there, you're going to wind up with an earful of cider.

1

Ambition Is What Makes Us Work Hard to Get Ahead; Greed Is the Other Fellow's Ambition

CON. *WEBSTER'S DICTIONARY* DEFINES "CON" AS "to learn, as in a lesson." *Webster's* also says something about "to trick and swindle," which gets down to where the water hits the wheel a whole lot better. I think it was Grandaddy's Rule #2 that said, You learn something new every day . . . unless you're very, very careful.

My old friend, realtor-consultant Hank Thompson, had a malfunctioning soda pop machine in the lobby of his building that regularly ate whatever coins it was fed and gave nothing in return. Over the coin-slot, Hank hung a small cardboard sign that read, Instant Teaching Machine: insert a quarter and learn a lesson.

The thesaurus equates "con" with "learning, as in self-instruction." Right next to that are the words "prevaricate," "garble," "gloss over," "cook up," and "concoct." These are easy enough to grasp.

Basically, a con is a con is a con. And Florida has always had a giant-sized helping of them all, throughout her four-hundred-year-plus history.

Florida scams, cons, stings, rip-offs, swindles . . . no matter what you hear them called, they range all the way from the simplest little-old-lady-pigeon-drops to the most complicated multi-million-dollar investment and stock market schemes. These include intricate bankruptcy scams involving folks with really deep pockets who seem to have a magic touch when it comes to financial maneuvering.

Often these deep-pocket folks simply want to have even *deeper* pockets, if they can get them. As you'll see, they often can—especially in Florida.

Florida, in some quarters, is known to be a bankruptcy haven. One state legislator, Senator Jim Scott, from the occasionally-maligned Fort Lauderdale, says that at least part of the blame must rest with the state legislature for being too easy on debtors and would-be bankruptcies coming to Florida. Florida's laws allow hundreds of bankrupt people to flee to the Sunshine State to escape their creditors in northern cities. (One of Grandaddy's Rules—I don't remember which one—said there was no danger in running into debt. It was running into your *creditors* that gave you problems.)

Anyway, the practice of declaring bankruptcy and running to Florida seems to be growing among the well-heeled crowd.

A bit north of Jim Scott's Fort Lauderdale, along Florida's magnetic southeastern Gold Coast, lies the famed city of Boca Raton, once nicknamed "Maggot Mile" in a *New York Times* News Service series.

It was here that Senator Scott addressed his fellow lawmakers, saying that while the legislature was busy with issues such as naming an official state pie, they should have been trying to close some of the loopholes in Florida's laws.

In 1993, even CBS's prestigious "60 Minutes" devoted a major story to Florida's generous tax exemption policies toward personal and corporate bankrupts from her northern neighbor states.

That story indicated that Florida had the longest list among all the fifty states of what a bankrupt person might keep, no matter how much he or she might owe to his or her creditors.

At that time, Senator Scott, "60 Minutes," and the respected Knight-Ridder area newspaper *The News* all made note of the organization Florida Taxwatch, Inc., a private, non-partisan, fiscal watchdog group based in Tallahassee. Taxwatch is also urging the state to clamp down on bankruptcy and tax-dodger cases.

While they may not be exactly big-league scams or cons in the strictest sense, both Taxwatch and "60 Minutes" cited the cases of baseball commissioner Bowie Kuhn and Ohio banker Marvin Warner.

According to the feature reports, Kuhn, within days of his law firm declaring bankruptcy in the north, moved to Florida, acquired a million-dollar home, and was reported to have brought a $2-million investment portfolio.

Warner, according to the stories, was able to scrape up enough to move to Florida and acquire a $3-million horse farm in the Ocala area after the collapse of his Cincinnati banking interests.

The end result of all scams, large and small, is that the little people get hurt. The little people are the ones who, through taxes, must eventually bear the burden of supporting all those who are able to avoid carrying their own fair share of the fiscal load. And these creative minds seldom run out of ideas on how to beat the system. They never exhaust their supply of assistants who conjure up various creative bookkeeping techniques.

And it's not only private individuals who cook up scams. You also get misappropriation of public monies, malfeasance in public office, and instances of frivolous or self-serving use of your money by bureaus and county commissions.

We'll be exploring all of the above and more, just ahead.

As every clean and decent, well-meaning con man or lady can tell you, there's always more than one way to skin a cat. And we'll find that, as stated in Grandaddy's Rules, If there exists a way to get around it, somebody, somewhere will *find* a way to get around it.

As the Taxwatch folks put it, quite succinctly, Florida should "stop letting the rich simply thumb their noses at the tax laws and at those to whom they owe lots of money."

But until some action is taken, Florida remains a magical place for con men, scammers, and folks who would like to duck their debts.

Speaking of magic, that brings us to Grandaddy's Rule #3: Nobody never pulled no rabbit out of no hat without carefully puttin' one in there first.

2

The Good Guys vs. the Bad Guys and Why They Both Love Florida

LET'S TALK ABOUT THESE SCAMS for just a moment. Let's explore what makes us tick and what makes scams and cons even possible—let alone probable.

There's a certain amount of what we might call Greed Factor in each of us; it's present in varying degrees of quantity and intensity. An old Florida land developer once said, "I don't want all the land, just a portion of whatever adjoins mine." It was a popular way of looking at things in the Florida of yesteryear, and it has carried over to the Florida of today.

A question people constantly ask about Florida is, Why are there so many scams? When you add up all of the state's assets, it's not too difficult to understand why.

Florida has amazing amounts of wondrous things: beautiful blue skies, golden sunshine, white sandy beaches, and emerald-green and crystal-blue waters.

Now all of these beautiful things, together on one grand stage, tend to attract a lot of people—about fifteen million or so at last count. And Florida will probably grow to twenty million in the new century. The state also has about a million visitors every weekend, just coming to pay their respects.

It's reasonable to assume that, with a base of fifteen

million folks, plus all those visitors, you're going to have an infinite variety of people. But for our purposes, we're going to divide all these citizens into just two main groups: the Good Guys and the Bad Guys.

Our first group, the Good Guys, will include the ma and pa from Omaha, the retired steelworker from Pittsburgh, the retired shoemaker from Massachusetts, the retired banker from New York, the retired fisherman from Muskegon, the retired tool-and-die maker from Toledo, and the retired grower from I-oh-way. Oh yes, and a whole bunch of youngsters who are not retired at all.

Now most of these folks are wonderful, down-to-earth, friendly old straight shooters. They're basic folks who have saved their hard-earned dollars for a lifetime so that they might have not just two glorious weeks in Florida each year, but "a little place of our own in Florida where the kids and grandkids can come and visit."

Our second group, the Bad Guys, will include the genuine con man from (insert your city of choice), the "investment counselor" from, oh, maybe Manhattan (the one in the black silk suit), the telephone hustler from Chicago, and an infinite variety of hustlers from Wherever, Utah. Pick a town; any town at all.

Florida simply—and eventually—gets them all.

This second group will also include the old-fashioned cardsharp, the grifter *and* the drifter, the phone boiler-room specialist . . . in short, just about every variety of operator you could think up, and many that we'd never dream of in a million years. Go back to Grandaddy's Rule # 2—the one that said you learn something new every day unless you're very, very careful. Remember?

Most of the time, it seems that for every member of the first group dedicated to holding on to their hard-earned dollars, there will be an opposite member of the second group, equally dedicated to *separating* the Good Guys from their money.

It's just as simple as that.

And it is to the first of these two groups that this book is addressed: to the Good Guys, may you continue to learn methods of holding on to your hard-earned bucks. May you develop your own personal basket of good old common sense, because the government can only do so much toward keeping you and your assets together. And the Bad Guys are going to remain just as dedicated to the premise that a fool and his money are soon parted.

Now some of Grandaddy's Rules are painfully simple. I've already given you a couple of them. And now, here's a couple new ones for you. (These don't have numbers.) Add: For every plus, somewhere there's a minus, and For every gain, somewhere there's a loss. Keep these in mind, and you'll generally be all right.

So make notes. Mark your pages if you need to. (It's your book.) The more dog-eared these pages become, the more you're going to learn how to gitalong.

Now how about those shady-but-charming characters coming in to Sunshine-land from California to New York, from Long Island to Austria, and all points in between. They've come to see if the grass really *is* greener in old Florida, as they've always heard.

When they look around, what do they find?

They find that golden sunshine I told you about; those fabulous moonlit nights; beautiful waters; and those *fifteen million folks,* ready and waiting. Probably half of these folks are in their mature years . . . maybe they're a little less sophisticated than they might once have been. They're now maybe a little more trusting of charming strangers; maybe a little more naive. All of this makes for a ripe harvest for those Bad Guys.

Really, who can blame them? Any self-respecting con man or lady is going to respond to that sort of stimuli when it is showcased in the beautiful setting of the Land of Eternal Sunshine. And these same con folk are going to take one look and say, Hey, all I want is a piece of whatever's next to mine.

So to the Bad Guys, all I can say is, Take your best shot. Because sooner or later, old Uncle Sam is going to nail you anyhow, on one thing or another—no matter how well you organize and execute. Of course, this doesn't always help the victimized Good Guys very much. But perhaps, once in a while, vengeance *may* be just a little bit sweet.

Back in the 1920s, during that wild ride on the land boom merry-go-round, Miami had a brand-new resident—a very substantial gent, said to have a personal income of $20 to $30 million per year. His business card read, Al Capone, Used Furniture Dealer. The furniture business had never been so good. Uncle Sam finally nailed him on income tax evasion.

So all things are possible.

As a matter of fact, the 1920s land boom was about to set a whole new moral standard for Florida con folk for generations to come. Some critics say that this madcap "Roaring Twenties Land Frenzy" became the Florida attitude for doing business for the next half-century.

It was this very attitude that helped lead Florida to the land abuses, high-pressure sales techniques, and conservationist vs. developer battles which grew all through the 1950s, '60s, '70s, and '80s.

From that powerful frenzy of the 1920s, equally powerful and vivid personalities had to come: the Mizners with their hypnotic dreams for Boca Raton; the old Oyster King, Willie Popham; "Dicky" Bolles and his invisible land; and the rip-off Rosens.

Sounds like a formidable lineup . . . and yet they only scratch the tip of the iceberg. Or whatever that simile is.

These people were just a handful of the trend-setters, the ones who garnered tons of printer's ink in worldwide headlines.

There were hundreds more who created smaller personal scams which skyrocketed to suck millions of dollars out of many local communities. A lot of these bucks came directly from the Good Guys, those friendly, unsuspecting, trusting seniors all over Florida.

Our odyssey through Florida's fifty-eight thousand square miles of scam land will bring us to almost every conceivable idea and scheme used by the Bad Guys to separate the Good Guys from their money.

We'll concentrate on no particular area or town, just wherever the scent of money takes us. Almost every square foot of Florida holds *some* attraction for the friendly hustler for one reason or another, so we'll try to be fair to all.

And remember, these pages are not intended to be judgmental in any sense of the word. Our courts will handle that role. No one is qualified to judge what motivates a fellow or gal to respond to a particular silver-tongued devil who's selling anvils or uniforms for a boys' band.

Always remember bank robber Willie Sutton's famous answer when he was asked, "Why do you rob banks?" It was (of course), "Because that's where the money is." We'll find that the action is usually wherever the money is. If this were not true, then Grandaddy's Rules (or at least Willie Sutton) would have told us so.

3

Prince Michael of Austria in Old Fort Lauderdale; or, The Bugattis Will Get You Every Time

As we travel the Scam Trail across the fifty-eight thousand square miles of Florida, we'll find a limitless selection of your average, everyday "scam du jours." We'll explore new and old cons, stings, and drops of almost every known variety—even those that seem to be harmless.

Occasionally we'll come across a scam that we'll have to categorize as image-building. Psychiatrists tell me that one of the forces that drives the industrious con man to create invisible empires—along with the obvious material rewards—is the desire to feel important, to elevate one's image, to rise above the rest of the group as a leader and model.

So, maybe, here's one of those.

As fearless investigative reporter-publisher Bernard McCormick reminds us, there was a time when dear old Fort Lauderdale had its own image problems. (Where the boys are, and all that.)

There was even a time when the "real hep guy," say from Youngstown, or Waterloo, or Boonville someplace, while heading to Florida for the winter party-time, would say, I'm heading for Fort Liquordale. (It was thought to be a very hip and clever line. Remember, it was the 1950s, so be gentle.)

And then, as McCormick relates, there was old Prince Michael of Austria, who invaded these shores sometime during the 1950s.

Prince Michael of Austria was an incredibly charming chap, as princes are liable to be. His charm was certainly not lost on the ladies, either. 'Nary a lady's hand would pass by him without a princely buss on the knuckles or fingertips.

These displays of continental gallantry, plus his savoir faire and his obvious trappings of immense, old world wealth, provided him entrée to the most gilded galas on the Gold Coast. Your ordinary, everyday, self-made millionaire from Milwaukee would have killed to have been invited to the soirees that literally demanded the presence of Prince Michael of Austria.

At these parties, Prince Michael of Austria would—are you ready?—occasionally go around *knighting* friendly guests. McCormick reports that the prince's buddies would actually become knights of the realm in the princely cadre back in old Hapsburg or Salzburg or Wartburg, or wherever he was from.

A little bit later, Prince Michael even began providing parchment certificates of the bearer's newfound knighthood.

The man was nothing less than astonishing. He became the newest star on the Fort Lauderdale social circuit more quickly than a Lauderdale native could say y'all.

Eventually, the prince's ever-widening circle of just a few hundred of his nearest and dearest friends learned that The Michael had some *other* wondrous talents, too.

Apparently, through certain of his mysterious, heraldic, ancient family connections, back at the Olde Familye Castle, the prince could get incredible—almost unbelievable—deals on fabulous European sports cars! He offered discounts like you just wouldn't believe!

Soon, members of the princely circle began sporting

glistening Alfa Romeos, Ferraris, Aston Martins . . . even an occasional antique Hispano Suiza, Dual Ghia or Bugatti! And all of them purchased at those unbelievable prices.

The pulse quickens . . . the blood races . . . reason totters. Listen, McCormick was *there!* He knew the prince *personally!* And he would have absolutely no reason to make the whole thing up.

As Mark Twain said, All men are like the moon. We all have a dark side we show to no one. So I suppose the Prince Charming stories must have a dark side, too.

In the midst of all the knuckle-kissing, Bugatti-delivering, knighting, and the like . . . while all this was going on in moonlight-drenched Fort Lauderdale, the Venice of America, well, guess what?

Some upstart young prosecuting attorney had the gall to stumble across some long-lost immigration records down at the customs office. And what do you know—the young attorney said that there was *no such person* as Prince Michael of Austria.

And *then* this young whippersnapper put some more pieces together and came up with the simply appalling suggestion that all those gleaming European sports cars gracing those paver-block driveways, overlooking the forty-foot Bertrams in the backyards of all those glistening Fort Lauderdale waterway mansions were *stolen!*

Well, *really!*

It seems that among his princely chums back in the Old World, there were several fun-loving mischief-makers who were known, occasionally, to purloin fancy cars from their owners' castles. These clever boys would then ship the cars overseas to contacts in the colonies, and eventually to Prince Michael in Fort Lauderdale. The prince could really move the goods and close the deals; he was a natural born closer.

Now, since there was no such person as Prince Michael of Austria, this fellow couldn't really *be* Prince Michael of

Austria after all, could he? He turned out to be a geek named Mike Walbaum from Toledo or Boston or maybe Philadelphia or someplace . . . (McCormick knows where he was from, I imagine). Anyway, it was some place a lot less mysterious and illustrious and Old Worldy than Vienna or Salzburg.

The cops didn't actually haul the prince off to the hoosegow, but the effect was pretty near the same. You could tell his princing days were coming to a close right smart.

When the gendarmes asked Walbaum why he would go to such extremes to become Prince Michael of Austria, he summed up the philosophy of the image-building con I told you about in very few words. He said, "Hey, who'd ever want to talk to some guy named Mike Walbaum from Toledo?"

And a lot of Lauderdale folks began to experience the faint sensation of just a drop or two of cider in the old ear. And they began to remember a few of Grandaddy's Rules—especially that old Rule #1 (the one that reminded you there ain't never nuthin' fer nuthin'). Just a glance at the price tags on the Ferrari or Aston Martin would have set Grandaddy's alarm bells a'ringing.

And those Lauderdale folks were about to learn a brand-new rule. It's called Grandaddy's Rule #4.

It began to gain stature during the Florida land boom when the slickers in the knickers began to work their famous land-selling hustle on the out-of-towners. (That's folks not from around here.)

If Papa Johnson were here today to tell it to them, he'd probably say, "If they's talkin' to you about pie in the sky, chances are they's gonna make it with your dough."

4

Joe the Piano Man and the Boiler-Room Boys

SPEAKING OF PRINCE MICHAEL OF AUSTRIA, you've probably never heard of Michael Krebser or Michael Spieles, either. These two would probably have to be classified as small potatoes con men. Although they had previous records involving a $20-million health insurance scam, their most recent con was only the old gold mine sting. The whole operation only nicked about $5 to $6 million or so out of 174 people. They got these people to invest their life savings into a supposed gold mine. Then, of course, Michael and Michael took all the money and split. It was small stuff.

That $20 mil that the Michaels had been working on—now that's real money. The little $6 mil scam was probably just to keep their hand in—you know, for practice.

But if Florida is going to retain her position as scam capital of the world, she must rely on these little guys with their little deals to keep things rolling along between the really giant cons produced by the major players.

It's just sort of the way things are in the scam bin-ness.

Maybe you heard about that guy selling those $5.42 tubes of toothpaste to the state's correctional institutions. This guy had a deal with the administration—honest—for almost $5.50 per tube. And the tubes even had their original ninety-seven-cent price tag right there on them.

The venerable paper *The Tampa Tribune* uncovered that one. The prisons said that the special toothpaste was ordered for Muslim inmates who claimed that all the other brands had some kind of pork derivative in them that was forbidden by their religion.

Anyway, as the story unfolded, amazingly enough, the corrections board apparently kept right on dealing with the same fellows. I guess they figured it had been a bookkeeping or price tag error, or something.

Now, how about those Florida charity fund-raisers? I mean the ones with the phone boiler-room operations that keep ninety-five cents out of every dollar they collect from the folks at the other end of the phone line, and only give about a nickel out of each dollar to the veteran's organization—or whatever—they represent.

And all of these are perfectly legal—sort of.

It's kind of a shock to learn that *some* charities actually *let* the phone-room boys keep up to 90 percent of all the funds they raise. It's even worse to hear that that's not enough for some operations—they want 95 percent! And they take it, laws or no laws.

Remember that the next time some suave, smooth-talking jasper on the telephone starts asking you to help lost kids save homeless cottonmouth moccasins.

Chances are that you'll never hear the company names behind the phone-room, or boiler-room, operations. There are more than *six thousand* operating in the country, creating very special headaches for state attorneys' offices and Better Business Bureaus all over.

Just imagine. Six thousand of those little boiler rooms all going full steam ahead, gradually separating about $800 million per year from unsuspecting folks, all for charity. Most of these funds turn out to be involved in outright fraud cases.

Of course, there are good phone operations, too, who have developed the buzzword "telemarketing," just as there are Good Guys and Bad Guys in almost every business.

As *Sun-Sentinel* business columnist Jack Nease points out, this troublesome boiler-room group skims (and skins) about two million folks every year in about forty-five of our states.

These good old boys' scams include—ready?—convincing some Wisconsin farmers to donate money to a fund to legalize cow growth hormones!

But when it comes to scams, Florida is, as Florida Attorney General Bob Butterworth said, "right up there near the top of the list."

South Florida's *Sun-Sentinel* Newspapers, in Broward and Palm Beach counties, produced an amazing series of investigative articles on boiler-room scams. The articles confirmed what authorities had long suspected: that Florida is a haven for phone hustlers. In, fact, the state has about three times as many problem phone-room operations as any other state in the nation. And Broward County itself appears to be an all-time favorite spot with the boiler-room boys.

In fact, Broward "telemarketers" were named in almost a third of the nearly fifteen thousand cases filed with the state since 1985, according to the *Sun-Sentinel,* and this number is nearly twice that of any other county in the Sunshine State.

And then there's Joe.

Joe, for heaven's sake, was just a good old piano man. That's right—he played piano on the condo circuit around the Fort Lauderdale scene.

According to the *Sun-Sentinel* stories, Joe apparently got to thinking that there must be an easier way to make a buck, even easier than playing piano for the condo folk. He later said that he didn't realize he was just a front man for a group of unidentified investors.

Anyway, Joe's organization sent out thousands of letters on letterhead with the name Clarke, Winston & Hayes, Ltd., of Phoenix. Pretty impressive right off, wouldn't you say?

The letters told their readers that a "search firm" had located lots of money that had been left in the New York State Comptroller's office by somebody with the same name as the person receiving the letter! And then the letter gave a 900 number for the reader to call to request forms for claiming the loot.

Now the readers didn't realize that the call entailed a $10 charge. But hey—getting all that loot is certainly worth a ten-spot. Except that Clarke, Winston & Hayes turned out not to exist at all. The Phoenix address turned out to be a mail drop, and the ten bucks simply went to the persons who installed the 900 number.

Old Joe had apparently just rented big random lists of names from folks who sell that sort of stuff to telemarketer firms. The articles say he even got AT&T to handle all the billing, placing the $10 charge on each caller's phone bill, and all. Joe was one persuasive, smart piano man.

With the electronic wonders of the 900-number system, this operation reached as far away as Iowa, where an assistant attorney general commented, "We've had more complaints on this scam than on any other 900 program in history." And remember folks, this was just a little one. Piano man Joe may still be tickling the ivories somewhere in Fort Lauderdale.

The *Sun-Sentinel* stories indicate that no one knows for sure just how much money is siphoned from Americans every year by all the different boiler-room artists. Some estimates have reached as high as *ten billion dollars.*

And while the newspaper's data banks have become one of America's most extensive repositories of information on such scams, the editors feel that they are still far from complete, and will probably just keep on growing.

5

The Incredible Parade of Purloining Personalities

WHILE ALL OF FLORIDA'S POSH SPAS and resorts provide varying degrees of attraction for the clear-thinking con man or lady, we have to start somewhere.

Among all those places, wherever your trust fund leads you—from Innisbrook to Ponte Vedra, from Seaside to Naples, from Miami Beach to Palm Beach, from St. Armand's to Sanibel, and all points in between—there is one town which appears to stand just a tad above the rest of the glittering group.

It's maybe just a tiny dab more enticing, attractive, tempting, and delicious. And that town is beautiful, charming, wealthy, exploding Boca Raton.

The city was virtually created by the 1920s land boom visionary Addison Mizner and his eccentric hustler brother Wilson. While Addison was sometimes referred to (by his competitors) as a genteel, suave con man, his brother had been a well-known gambler and hustler, involved in more than a few major league schemes during his career as a promotion man. (He would tour the country promoting a dancing—or boxing—bear, or the like.)

And since it was during America's heady, adolescent Roaring Twenties *and* Florida's very own madcap, wild and crazy land boom, the Mizners and their seventeen-thousand-acre dream city fit right in.

It was during this period that the frenzied, land-grabbing attitude I referred to in chapter two was established. This helped set the scene for scams to become so widespread in Florida. The con men were ordering in several decades' worth of cider.

The Mizners, during the romping, stomping days of the land boom, promoted their dream city as "part Venice, part Paris, and part Paradise," the "grandest in the universe!" And today's Boca Raton surely seems—finally—to have it all. It at least has more than enough of the necessary ingredients to attract the modern-day con man or lady.

Boca Raton has attracted hordes of the Beautiful People—many thousands of them—who are young, extremely well-to-do, very upwardly-mobile, and nearly always interested in a very good deal (especially a deal that might make them tons of money quickly).

As one old-timer (a guy about forty-five) said down at the tennis courts, "I'm not criticizing all this. I just want to get *in* on a little of it."

Mix the Beautiful People (and their money) with the con men, and you have the recipe for ventures of all kinds. They show up in headline after headline: "Eleven Locals Held in $10 Million Collections Scam;" "Where Is Cascades Chairman Incendy?;" "College Bound Inquiry;" "Oil and Gas Wells Limited Partnership Explodes;" and countless others.

It is imperative to understand that any community that is highly attractive to well-to-do young professionals, to new businesses, to major national and international corporations, and to the retired folks, is bound to be equally attractive to the Bad Guys.

And remember, these are not your average, everyday, "pea-under-the-walnut-shell" con folk. These are major-league specialists who garner major-league profits and major-league print space, tube time, and sound bites in the nation's media.

It is not unusual to be able to study two or three major investigations going on at any given moment in these rich, fertile fields of Florida.

In fact, within a single week's time, an investigative reporting crew and Ms. Sarah Ragland of the *Sun-Sentinel* developed stories that seemed to tumble one after the other. One story was about a call-in phone service hustle that would let you hear from a serial killer at $1.99 per minute. (Assuming you might want to hear from a serial killer at all, at any price.)

A second major scam was underway at the same time, promising untold riches via owning your own pizza-vending machines (or something like that). And a third scam was also using the phones, promising to help you sell your time-share unit (another happy-go-lucky Florida product from the Swinging '70s) for a fat fee.

There was also that case about the diet products, which were promoted as being endorsed by a panel of four physicians. Reports on all the talk shows and in business news columns revealed that two of the doctors involved apparently weren't even licensed to practice in Florida. The third physician was under investigation for malpractice . . . and the fourth fellow unfortunately had died a couple of seasons earlier. (Got to remember to get those letterheads changed.)

These are still just the tip of the iceberg.

As respected Chamber of Commerce President Mike Arts put it, "We are victims of our own success." City Council member Steven Abrams said that while other towns may have scams and frauds, they're just not quite as sophisticated. He said, "Other towns might have a 'resurface-the-driveway' scam while we seem to attract these elaborate telemarketing schemes." It's truly fascinating to watch from the sidelines.

Addison Mizner would have been impressed.

Wilson Mizner would have loved it.

In another instance, even the eminent *New York Times* News Service, with Ms. Diana Henriques, paid a visit to town, exploring "Boca's Bogus Businesses." The article, reprinted in area newspapers, explored no less than *five* firms, all being investigated at the same time by various bodies.

Companies providing lead stories for the business media include College Bound, a chain of scholastic-testing coaching centers which had been a stock market darling in 1993; Cascades International, with its missing chairman and CEO, Victor Incendy; Great Oaks Financial, undergoing an SEC investigation; and Ringside International, an inactive boxing promotion company, among others.

Mike Arts commented, "We don't have the luxury of picking and choosing our residents. . . . Our unemployment rate is consistently under five percent. And we've often announced more new companies here [in Boca Raton] within a single year than some entire states have done."

And as Vice Mayor and Councilperson Wanda Thayer (a native from the Gainesville area) stated, "Boca Raton, in the corporate world, is a very attractive address."

And we haven't even gotten to Thomas Mullens and his Omni Capital Group yet. Nor have we touched on the rest of Florida's fifty-eight thousand square miles, eleven hundred towns and cities, and fifteen million people, either. But they're coming right up (some of them, anyway). All this geography takes a while to cover.

Let's just check around in Boca Raton for a few more of the fairly current operations before we hit the road. (You may want to make notes in case one of these should call on you someday.)

Here's a nifty one. How about the Single's Choice Dating Service! This operation sold itself as "the elusive secret to social success"! (Exclamation point is my own.) The service encouraged young singles (probably preferring well-heeled ones) to drop by and fill out a questionnaire. So far, no problem. But *aha!* The plot begins to thicken, and the cider begins to bubble in the vat.

Somehow—and I still can't figure this one out—the operators end up with the prospect's *credit card!* (Remember your Key Word List that you started with "leaving" in the Introduction? Add "credit card" to it. Never, never, never give it out!)

The credit cards ended up with *hu-mong-us* (local phrase) charges on them. Even the authorities are still trying to figure out how this one worked, so we shouldn't feel too bad if we don't get it.

Maybe you had to be an attractive, well-heeled, young single person to understand it all.

That *New York Times* News Service story reminded folks that in this exquisite, exclusive spot, dozens of "companies" may simply be corporate shells created by boiler-room brokers, whose chief products would appear to be their own news releases boasting of so-called prospects, imaginary sales, and nonexistent profits, rather than any actual earnings.

It was here, in good old naive Florida, that Preacher Robinson developed his saying that became Grandaddy's Rule #5 (Papa Johnson's favorite). At the church suppers out on the beach, Preacher Robinson used to say, "I wanna be around when the meek inherit the earth, so I can watch the *un-meek* take it away from 'em."

6

The Open Road to Scam Land and the $50 Tipper in the Rolls

IN THE MIDDLE OF THE excitement chamber that was chapter five, we mentioned that we hadn't even gotten to Thomas Mullens and his Omni Capital Group yet.

Well sir, the time has come.

As *The New York Times* News Service story relates, Mr. Mullens, chairman of Omni Capital Group, was a popular golfer around town and a Chamber of Commerce member. His regular Friday schedule included driving his Rolls to Bruno's Hair Salon for a trim and manicure, where he would leave his customary $50 tip. Now, even in Boca—heck, even *"in season"*—this sort of behavior will get you in the public eye more quickly than a Noo York minute. (Papa Knight used to say, the orange gets all the publicity but it took the grapefruit to get in the public eye.)

Soon, the barber was impressed enough to invest some $45,000 with this fellow in his investment company. He also got investments from members of his golfing crowd, plus a hundred or so retired couples in the area.

Sure enough, the end result was that the fellow was eventually arrested and indicted on running a "Ponzi" scheme. It might wind up costing the investors in the neighborhood of some $10 million. (That's a pretty expensive neighborhood.)

Now just so we'll all be on the same page, a Ponzi scheme, in its barest essentials, means that a promoter is selling shares in something. It was named for the brilliant con artist who thought it up. It's also called a "pyramid" scheme.

Here's how it works:

First, the promoter tells the prospect that he or she is going to earn a *guaranteed* (another Key Word for your list) return of 29 percent on their investment each year. At this point, a small bell should start ringing in the prospect's brain and visions of cider should start dancing around in his or her head.

Next, the prospect, ignoring the bell, buys $20,000 worth of shares, or maybe $200,000, depending on your part of town and where you get your haircuts.

Then the prospect actually *does* get a 29 percent dividend following the first quarter or first year earnings statement. (The ringing gets louder, but the prospect is deafened by joy and pays no attention.) The prospect decides, I'm really on to something! This guy really knows his potatoes!

The prospect now goes to his hidden cache of golf-bet money in the mayonnaise jar, or to the sock under the bed where he hides it from the missus . . . or maybe even to some of his pension-fund money, if he has decided to become a really major player. The prospect has now decided that the streets are indeed paved with gold.

The promoter, at this point, is actually paying "dividends" on the prospect's first investment from the proceeds of his sales to *other prospects.* In terminal cases, the promoter may be paying dividends on that first sale out of proceeds from the *second* sale to the *original* prospect.

This means that any "earnings" are often simply portions of the prospect's own money being given back to him (or her) as "dividends." As our astute, mature, well-advised, and sophisticated investor will quickly discern, and as attorney Robert Rex points out, this simply amounts to a return *of* your investment, rather than a return *on* your investment.

At this point, the house of cards is about to tumble, leaving the jack of spades soaring into the stratosphere and squirting cider every whichaway.

It just can't *not* happen.

Obviously, in this, as in all variations of this pyramid sales plan, dividends and returns are derived only from continuing to make sales to new prospects.

It's sort of like the way any out-of-power political party refers to our Social Security system: each new generation of buyers is expected to pick up the tab for the previous generation.

While there are literally countless variations on this scheme, the basic technique always remains the same: they pay returns to the first investors from the proceeds of sales to later customers.

Those little warning bells should always be tinkling merrily whenever somebody offers you what seems to be something for nothing (Grandaddy's Rule #1). Or when they offer a deal that really seems too good to be true, which brings us to Grandaddy's Rule #6: If it *seems* too good to be true, chances are, it is.

Now before we move on, there are just a few more items on our agenda that we should review. And these are biggies, so hang on.

In another instance told to me by friendly barrister Robert Rex, it just happens that a lot of Boca folks were among the 120,000 U.S. investors who bought into that truly major-league plan, the Prudential Energy Limited Partnership, back in the 1980s.

According to countless print, radio, and TV stories, the Prudential Securities Energy unit sales were reported to total more than a *billion* dollars in the oil and gas limited partnerships.

The New York Times reporter Kurt Eichenwald produced an entire *book* on the Pru-Bache Securities situation.

Eichenwald's title, *Serpent on the Rock,* tells volumes about the content.

In this work, he figures the number of injured investors at about 340,000 (instead of 120,000). This includes about 70,000 friendly seniors in the Sunshine State.

Eichenwald's estimate of the total losses suffered by the victims of the scam multiplies the previous $1 billion eight times over, soaring to around $8 billion.

Eichenwald pulls no punches in describing limousines, luncheons, parties, hunting trips, wine cellars, sales incentive ocean cruises . . . he even itemizes lobsters, steaks, cigars, and wine at dinners for company execs . . . all partially provided by charges to investors' accounts.

On one of Eichenwald's visits to Boca Raton, he indicated that new federal legislation might make it even more difficult for the small investor to seek redress against any giant operator. The new proposed rules would mean that the investor would have to prove that an operator *knew* a venture was going to fail, and was actually intending to commit fraud—a virtually impossible task.

Eichenwald describes a Pru-Bache executive directive to its brokers which tells it all: "New York picks the products. Your job is to sell them, not examine them or ask questions. Just sell them."

The end result? The total invested capital of the 340,000 investors was said to have dwindled to less than 50 percent of its original value.

Many of the partnerships had soured, triggering countless lawsuits by investors, which eventually led to a 120,000-member class action suit filed in a New Orleans court on behalf of many of the investors.

There were some two hundred Palm Beach County folks who are said to have joined in the suit. After hard analysis, a proposed settlement offered by the defendant was estimated to produce about a penny on the dollar for the claimants in return for their losses.

Following this revelation, some of the attorneys and clients decided to exclude themselves from the class-action suit and to file individual suits for their losses.

Attorney Rex indicates that sometimes individual plaintiffs fare better by pursuing an action on their own, rather than through a class-action suit. He adds that, in a case of this dimension—120,000 plaintiffs—one of the single suits might develop into a multi-million-dollar case on its own (perhaps a retired couple seeking to recover their entire life savings).

The investment sales operations and the nationwide telephone boiler-room techniques are often aimed directly at the senior citizens. As we will explore later, these are the ones who often prove to be the most trusting, susceptible, vulnerable prospects.

By the 1990s, with at least one quarter of Florida's nearly fifteen million folks fitting into the senior citizen category, there would appear to be a definite need for caring lawyers who specialize in helping senior scam victims.

One last note. Counselor Rex tells us that, as the oil and gas limited partnerships began to run out of steam, an amazing new development began to take shape in Boca Raton.

Some of the sales agents, in addressing disgruntled investors, recommended that some of their funds be placed in another investment plan. It was local and well-known, and therefore probably pretty reliable.

They suggested that the funds be placed in the care of a smooth-talking, good-looking local fellow. Good golfer, Chamber of Commerce member, drove a big Rolls down to the old barbershop every Friday morning and handed out $50 tips to the boys. Maybe you heard about him . . . quite a guy.

These folks were about to get *more* cider in their ears.

7

The Old Hidden Treasure Ploy and the "Dicky" Bolles Disappearing Land Auction

AS WE ARE RAPIDLY DISCOVERING, there is really no end to the number and variety of scams from which to choose. We may search from the famed 1920s land boom when Florida first discovered that she could sell land by the gallon . . . to the Mizner dream city of Boca Raton . . . to the hidden treasure ploy of Treasure Island and other cities; we'll simply never run out of scams.

Take the '20s land boom era alone, with its economic euphoria fostered by newly-arrived prospects carrying satchels filled with ready cash. Add to this the devil-may-care philosophy of the time, and you have the perfect spawning grounds for scams of just about every conceivable type.

All of these were aimed, simply, at separating the prospective land-buyers from some of their dough. (See Grandaddy's Rule #4, the pie in the sky one.)

One of the simplest cons used in selling real estate during the boom was the old Hidden Treasure Ploy.

In this scam, a developer would spread rumors of ancient pirate treasure buried somewhere near his location. This would attract hordes of treasure hunters, plus some prospective land-buyers, and even some plain old curious local folk.

Hey, we natives thought this was pretty exciting stuff. You don't have to go getting high and mighty on *us*. We weren't going to buy anything anyhow. That was just for the Northern folks and the out-of-towners.

The hidden treasure ploy was simple and easy, and it required no cash outlay of any kind. These were all qualities which appealed strongly to the land boom promoters.

The ploy's effectiveness seemed to grow with use. It was tried by a developer outside of Miami in 1923 . . . worked like a charm. Another land promoter repeated it several times along the lower Gold Coast . . . it continued to draw crowds. The scam spread across the state, along the Gulf Coast, into the Tampa Bay area, and kept on working.

Folks promoting the old Ransom E. Olds town of Oldsmar, near the north tip of Tampa Bay, pulled a switcheroo and changed it to a "phantom *gold* strike!" Folks flocked to the area to begin panning for gold they had heard rumors about. The folks poured in, but the gold didn't.

Across the bay, the hidden treasure gambit was said to have played a small part in the actual naming and creation of the present-day city of Treasure Island at the western edge of the Pinellas Peninsula/St. Petersburg region.

Here, Noel Mitchell put it all together. Now Noel was an interesting guy, a real go-getter. He didn't lay $50 tips on the boys down at the barber shop, but this was the Gulf side of Florida, and it was only the 1920s. Fifty bucks was a lot of money! Heck, Mitchell probably bought some of his waterfront lots for fifty bucks.

Anyway, Noel floated a rumor way back in 1913, before the big boom was about to start. The rumor said that buried treasure was to be found on his island. Mitchell hoped that the rumor would promote lot sales for the island development. The scheme failed to fool canny (1913) St. Pete natives, but the name caught on.

The hidden treasure con also attracted treasure-seekers

to an area near the western end of the then-new Gandy Bridge linking St. Petersburg and Tampa.

Rumors told of a vast store of treasure buried in an obscure, swampy, island-development-to-be. Folks came, they saw, they dug. The wind left the sails of the scheme when a treasure-hunter team unearthed—are you ready?—a dirty, beat-up, old *golf bag*—and not even one with any clubs in it.

As Broward historian, author Stu McIver, tells, the hidden treasure ploy was even tried by the amazing Mizners in the massive promotion of their Boca Raton dream city.

At one point in their sales campaign, Wilson Mizner, the fun-loving scamp brother, and publicist Harry Reichenbach were said to have planted some old coins in the sand along Boca's beachfront and inlet land. They then carefully leaked the rumor that ancient pirate treasure was to found in that area. But they found that they didn't need the treasure ploy, as their land sales averaged two million (1925) dollars *per week* at the zenith.

I guess we should, after all, name Wilson Mizner as our Hustler Emeritus Laureate. For although Florida did not spawn the affable rascal, she did provide him with his grandest stage: the Mizner dream city, with the entire Florida land boom as a golden-curtained backdrop.

Wilson had run the gamut from taking part in the "old badger game" in Alaska to running illegal gambling joints around the country; from cardsharping on luxury liners to touring the Rocky Mountains managing a trained bear as a boxer. Now that last feat should certainly qualify him!

As McIver says in his *Glimpses of South Florida History,* it was thus that Wilson Mizner belonged in Florida. It was preordained that he be a part of the land boom, which was the promoter's dream come true.

With Addison Mizner as the dynamic, visionary leader, and con man brother Wilson promoting the whole shebang, little was ever heard of their third brother, an

Episcopalian priest who got his siblings to scavenge scrap materials to build a small chapel so that their mother might attend services there. (As you may recall, Adam and Eve had a third son who got into no trouble at all, so hardly anyone ever heard anything about him, either.)

McIver adds another chapter to our story of scams: the famous, historic Frank Oliver House—home of the scam on the New River in Fort Lauderdale.

In this case, again during the 1920s, a group of well-dressed, smooth-talking jaspers set up telephone lines in the historic old Oliver house so that they could run a fake bookie operation inside. (Remember, that's a *fake* bookie operation—sort of a scam-of-a-scam.)

In this case, the customers would be told by pretty girls (these fellows didn't leave anything to chance) that the house had tapped wires that provided racing results sooner than the other horse parlors and bookie joints would get them. (Now stay with us, because this gets a little complicated as we go along.)

The customers, or "marks," would be "sandbagged." (Which is certainly a time-honored, traditional technique in such goings-on, just like your buddy does his golf handicap. We surely can't fault these hustlers for that.) The marks would be allowed several juicy but modest wins, building them up for a major bet, a giant, sure-thing "killing." Only thing was, a bet of this magnitude would have to be placed at the headquarters, in New Orleans. (Hey, you can almost feel that cider in your ear, can't you?)

Well sir, on the train traveling to New Orleans to place that bet, the pro who was accompanying the mark (and who was carrying the satchel full of his betting cash, we may be sure) would have to go to the bathroom, or something . . . and would simply disappear—with the money. (No matter what the technique or circumstance, this maneuver still falls under the heading of "leaving" in your Key Words List.)

If all of the foregoing seems hauntingly familiar to you, it should. As McIver relates, the entire scenario could have been the plot for the much later bookie scam immortalized in the Paul Newman/Robert Redford classic movie "The Sting." Only this scenario was real.

McIver adds a third tale of intrigue with the saga of old Richard "Dicky" Bolles . . . a tale that goes back to 1911, but echoes into the 1990s.

Realtor/developer/promoter Bolles was a man well ahead of his time. He belonged to the 1920s land boom, but he began his operations a whole decade before the rest of the guys.

Bolles actually created an entire make-believe town in the Fort Lauderdale area in 1911. His town attracted more than three thousand people to a single week-long land-buying frenzy; busses brought them in from the midwest while "closers" pumped them up all along the way, probably getting them all swimmy-headed with free hot-dogs and soda pop.

Bolles had a half-million acres to sell which he had just bought from the state at fifty cents an acre, so he had a lot of room to play with. He came up with an incredible idea: a combination land promotion, auction, and downright lottery. Listen to this one!

Folks were convinced to buy a $240 "lottery ticket," which, when drawn, would let them in on the "auction." Here, they would be allowed to bid on the lot of their choice. (Now try to follow me through on this, because here's where it gets interesting. This guy Bolles was really a thinker.)

The folks were then told to bid exactly $240 for their lot. *And* they were told that nobody else would bid against them. So the idea was that they would get their lot for the price of their lottery ticket, and come out an absolute winner. Remember, Bolles had bought the lots for *fifty cents an acre!* With three to four lots per acre, at $240 for a lot, his return would be about a quad-zidrillion percent for his weekend's work.

Anyway, at least Dicky Bolles had it figured out, even if nobody else could understand it. And it was his game.

Trainloads of folks poured into "Progreso" (the name of the dream town just north and west of today's Fort Lauderdale). It became an instant, sprawling tent city for the 1911 land-buyers, who were all scrambling for lots in the new town. The town had been variously described as a "promised land," a "land of destiny," and a "tropical paradise."

For one frenzied weekend, folks just couldn't seem to get enough of Progreso as they gobbled up residential lots.

"Dicky" had a hit on his hands.

As Monday rolled around, folks went out to look at the lots they had "won." (They were probably feeling secretly smug.)

And now comes the cider.

The folks suddenly realized that *they couldn't find their land!*

"Dicky" Bolles, inventive, creative promoter that he was, had single-handedly pioneered the treasured land boom innovation of selling land by the gallon. The customers' "glorious residential lots" were mostly lying under acres and acres of murky, weedy, muddy, dark, forbidding Florida swamp.

Bolles and his top men were all arrested and indicted on twelve counts covering a wide variety of charges. Hey! In this landmark case, even their *lawyer* was arrested. How about *that*, sports fans!

But eventually all the charges were dropped. Bolles faded into relative obscurity.

The Bolles lottery technique lived on in major land development sales well into the '70s and '80s. Even in the 1990s, the Federal Communications Commission tried a lottery as a means to award hundreds of millions of dollars in media licenses. This last venture also "came a cropper," as many bidders, winning the initial bid for licenses, simply defaulted and failed to come up with the major down payment on their newly-found cash cows.

8

Neal Anthony and the B.R.A.A. Secret Society—and More of the Incredible Parade of Purloining Personalities

BY THE WAY, ONE MORE ITEM or so before we leave that oil and gas limited partnership scene. The national business press, radio and TV talk shows, and trade journals all indicated that Prudential Securities projected that a total cost for the limited partnership debacle might eventually be in excess of $1.1 *billion.* As the grand old Speaker of the House Sam Rayburn used to say, "A billion here, a billion there, first thing you know, you're talking about real money."

While reports differed on the projected total costs, and they continue to do so even at this writing, this one billion figure would make the event one of the most costly investment scandals in Wall Street history—and certainly far and away the Florida winner of all time.

Maybe you *can* fool all of the people all of the time.

Just about everybody seems to have ideas on whether—and why—Florida should be named the world capital of scam, and how she grew to such prominence in the first place.

Some say it's the climate, the moonlit nights, the tropical breezes that drive men balmy and turn on their greed hormones. (I made that one up. There is no medical record of anyone ever having greed hormones. But it could happen.)

Other wise critics say it is simply the availability of easy money . . . and so much of it!

Jim Driscoll of the *Sun-Sentinel* Newspapers said, "She's a crazy-quilt state, Florida is. Maybe the complex makeup of her people is such that it simply provides a magnet for those seeking to pluck an easy buck from the unsuspecting."

Some think that it began with Florida's early pioneer, swashbuckling pirate, land baron, empire-building days—a time when men dealt in thousands, even millions of acres of land. Eminent business columnist Jack Nease once put these good folk into his "IGM club:" the I-Got-Mine guys. And some of them, or at least some of their philosophical descendants, are still with us.

And new ones are arriving almost every day.

Other commentators point to the laissez-faire attitude of various state governments over the centuries as the key ingredient. Let's check that out.

Now we can take this ride just about as far back as you'd care to go. How about the old Florida Internal Improvements Commission—ever hear of that one? That was a group of well-meaning political appointees who served on a big committee. Their main job was awarding contracts to railroad-builders starting back in the 1850s or so. They also gave the rail-builders state land as "right-of-way" land for the tracks. This right-of-way land lay alongside the tracks. (Now make a note that these old train tracks were about four or five feet apart.)

Anyway, that was the job of this Internal Improvements Commission: to award the land to the rail-builders in return for their promise to build some railroads.

Certainly seems simple enough so far, doesn't it?

Anyway, these good old boys were busier than a bee in a tarbucket, just awarding land left and right to the railroad companies who were promising to build some of Florida's first railroads. (She didn't have hardly any at all up 'til then and she really, really, really needed some.) So they all figured they'd be way ahead, no matter what the deal was.

Well sir, first thing you know, they started awarding "bonuses" of land as an added incentive to the rail folks to really get them going on building those railroads.

Hey, this was in the 1850s, and life was simpler then. (You do somebody a favor, and you'd expect to get one back.)

Well now, next thing you know, this little old Internal Improvements Commission is handing out *miles* of land to the railroad guys, and some of them hadn't driven that first spike yet.

And then, the railroad owners are collecting up to six to eight *miles* of right-of-way lands (wide) for every one mile length of track they were *promising* to put down.

But wait. It gets better, directly.

Well sir, when it got right down to where the water hit the wheel, it turned out that two of the five committee members—you know, the group handing out the six-to-eight-mile-wide swaths of land for those five-foot-wide rails—the fellows *awarding* the land goodies to the railroad companies—were the *presidents* of the rail companies that were *receiving* the goodies.

They were actually awarding millions of acres of land to their own companies. The companies would then almost immediately turn it over to a land development company—or to their own land company—which would broker huge tracts to other developers, and so on down the line. What a scam!

Now, remember Neal Anthony? The city of Tamarac does.

And the town will someday probably be asked to erect a statue in honor of Neal—as well they should.

In case you don't remember, Neal was the guy who proclaimed himself national president, founder, board member, chairman, director, and probably only member of B.R.A.A. (It was not an organization supporting foundation garments.)

Neal's group was eventually revealed to be the Bamboozled Retirees Association of America.

Neal was simply a guy who believed in standing up for his

rights. He got into a pretty nasty dispute with his condominium association. (I don't expect that they realized what kind of tiger they had by the tail.) He finally filed a court case to fight his condo developers; he said they were scamming him.

Neal stated that they had tried to hornswoggle him into signing a *fifty-year* contract for various services and for the use of his condominium common areas and its reception facility. Neal figured that fifty years seemed like a heck of a long time for such a document as that, and he told them so, in no uncertain terms.

He even planned a one-man protest march; he was going to march all around the condo carrying big signs and all, protesting that fifty-year contract.

The only problem arose when Neal's doctor told him he shouldn't do it; he said he shouldn't get so worked up about things—especially just when he was approaching his ninetieth birthday.

So let's hear it for Neal Anthony and the Bamboozled Retirees Association of America—and for Grandaddy's Rule #5—the one about the meek inheriting the earth and the un-meek taking it away from them.

We hope all your Florida days will be sunny ones . . . and, as you slide down the banister of life, may the splinters always be going your way . . . and sur'an' may you be sitting at the right hand of your maker an hour and a half a'fore th' divil even knows you've gone . . . and all the rest of those great toasts from our Irish cracker friends.

But be sure to remember Grandaddy's Rule #7—a new one to add to your list, along with those Key Words to watch out for: it's that golden rule about doing your bin-ness in the Deep South and it comes down to us from ancient anthropology. It says: Man will not eat his own kind. He will, hy-ever, skin 'em.

And if a Florida scam ever comes your way, those will prove to be mighty good words to live by.

9

Congratulations! You've Won the Billion-Dollar Lottery! Now You Can Pay Off Your Car Note!

THE FLORIDA LOTTERY HAS BECOME a target of scam operations—sometimes with tragic results not normally part of the scam games. In Miami, an elderly man, upon learning that he had been duped out of his life savings of $7,000 in a lottery ticket scam, drove his car into a deep canal and drowned.

Investigators indicate that the lotto ticket scam is not uncommon, especially in neighborhoods that are known to include foreign-born or elderly residents.

In what has been termed one of the biggest of all Florida lotto scams, Florida Attorney General Bob Butterworth filed a civil suit against the "Florida Club." Butterworth's office said that the club operators told customers that, for a fee, they and other members of the club would split the winnings—millions—if they ever won the lottery. It probably seemed like a fun idea, and that nobody could possibly get hurt. After all, *somebody's* got to win the thing.

It was the same sort of deal you have down at the office where you all go in together and buy some tickets; these folks were just selling "memberships" in a "lottery club."

The phone sales hustlers would wait 'til the lottery jackpot grew to those tantalizing, magic, high numbers, and then they'd go to work. (Now these were the real pros—the ones who could convince you that not only were their grapefruit so big it only took eight of them to make a dozen, but also that their eggs were so fresh, the hen hadn't even missed them yet. That's high-powered selling.)

Anyway, these major-league closers would call all over the country, selling memberships in the club. They would often specialize in calling states that had no lottery.

Prospects were told that for a $99.90 membership fee, their money and that of forty-nine other members would go in a pool to buy 904 lottery tickets at $1 each. If they won, each member would get 2 percent of the jackpot.

The prospects of winning were so exciting, so mouth-watering, that apparently nobody ever thought to whip out a calculator and do some figuring with those numbers.

Then the club actually won a $29-million jackpot. And the members started watching their mailboxes for their checks, figuring on about $590,000 each.

Here comes the jack of spades with his cider jug.

The members were told that they would only get about $300,000 each, and that the remainder of the money was to go to the promoter of the club for expenses and stuff.

At this point, members began to get steamed, and began burning up the phone lines to Bob Butterworth's office in Tallahassee. An investigation was immediately launched, and a suit was filed.

The paid-in members should have seen the light long before the drawing took place. Since there were fifty folks paying $99.90 each for their memberships, that would come to about $4,995 . . . which apparently was only going to produce a total of 904 tickets at $1.00 each. Now *that* is fascinating arithmetic. (Watch my hands closely at all times, folks.)

Somebody should have remembered Will Rogers's famous credo: I never believe anything I hear and only half of what I see.

The explanation was that the members had only been

buying "half-tickets," or something like that—*and* that the promoter had been actually holding on to a fifty percent interest in the club. (It still didn't come out right, and I'm not sure I ever did get it, even when it was explained to me.)

There seems to be no end to the variations on the good old simple ways of doing your scam bin-ness. A Miami company was contracted to move debris away and clean up after Hurricane Andrew hit town in 1992. They were paid about $15 million for the job. The company was found to have been just shifting giant piles of trash from one South Dade County site to another, sort of shuffling the monster piles of debris around, instead of hauling them away.

Investigators of this scam reported that much of the trash was simply left to rot in various areas of South Dade County.

And that's where Grandaddy's Rule #8 comes in.

As countless editorials, talk shows, and press stories constantly remind Florida folks, and all of us, for that matter, when it comes to a flier, handbill, free ticket, brochure, agreement, or contract . . . sooner or later, we have to use common sense and *read* that sucker. Read *all* the print on both sides of the paper. (That's assuming you even *got* a piece of paper. If you didn't, well, you're really in trouble.)

Because it's always true that, as Grandaddy's Rule #8 says, The large print giveth and the small print taketh away.

10

The Siding Game Comes to Old Winter Haven; or, I'd Give a Thousand Dollars to Be a Millionaire

THERE'S A FASCINATING ASPECT OF Florida scams. It seems that just about every town has its own personal, private, local, home-grown scam. And the deeper you probe, the more it seems that each town shows almost a certain pride in its own local scam.

Scam. Mention the word in any barbershop in any town from Marianna to Milton to Madison to Sarasota to Dade City . . . go ahead, try it. The town barbershop is where it all happens. And you're going to get answers including, "Well, we got one of the biggies," and, "yep, we got them all," and, "yes sir, you've come to the right place, all right," and words to that effect. Each town is downright proud of its own accomplishments in the scam bin-ness.

Now Winter Haven is a wonderful place. It has pretty lakes, rolling hills, nice people, and some good old boy families to give it F.S. (Florida Substance).

It also helped produce one of the grandest scams in all Florida. Not necessarily huge, say, by Boca standards, but full of down-home quality. It's a locally-bred type of scam, the kind you could only get in a community where just about everybody knows everybody and folks call you by name when you pass them on the street—or down at the barbershop.

Winter Haven has a certain friendliness, a charm that's

kind of hard to describe—or to resist. Even the name sings to the traveler . . . and has, probably clear back to when old man Eyclesheimer first named the place.

There it was, nestled among the nice, rolling hills . . . mixed in with all those little lakes. The place was always considered a haven from Old Man Winter.

Presto! Winter Haven.

Mr. Eyclesheimer probably would have loved my grandaddies and their rules.

Now in just about every town in Florida, you'll also find a cluster of Old Families. These are the names you'll see on old buildings, street signs, banks, and other pioneer businesses. Scratch some paint on an old building and you might even find a livery stable, a blacksmith, or a tavern.

And in just about every pioneer family, if you go back, say three generations or more, you're going to find all types of "young'uns," including a willful son or daughter who simply insisted on marching to his or her own (different) drummer.

According to our barbershop correspondents, a certain young man named Steve would have been kind of like that.

Steve's family had come to Winter Haven a long, long time ago . . . settled in the town, got started in bin-ness . . . their various sons and daughters grew . . .

And then along came Steve.

Steve was the bright, good-looking, and motivated grandson who marched to his own drummer. He felt the world was his oyster, just there for the taking. Folks who knew Steve as a kid said that this young man was always dressed for a parade; he was really going places. He was going to amount to something.

Steve sort of grew up in the business world. He was a comer. He did well at his jobs, made a few bucks, and everything was going along just hunky-dory. He was one of those fellows who could sell those "eight-grapefruit dozens" by the dozen, I guess you could say.

And then Steve got the Idea.

The Idea was really kind of simple. As most folks now understand—in hindsight—the Idea was to sell some shares in some oil wells, I think it was, sort of guaranteeing buyers a fixed return on their investment. But the really clever part of the Idea was that Steve figured out they could probably pay that fixed return to the first folks from the proceeds of sales to the *next* folks. Hey! Is that creative financing or what? Sound familiar?

And you know, Steve and the fellows probably never even gave a second thought to the fact that they were just working another variation of the old pyramid scheme.

Anyway, it worked out okay for awhile. Young Steve was so well-known, what with his family being there for generations and all, that folks just naturally gravitated toward the young bucko and assumed he had a real good thing going for him . . . and for them, too.

It was almost like that $50 tipper in the Rolls down at the barbershop in Boca Raton, except for those $50 tips. (The $50 tips probably wouldn't have gone over well in Winter Haven, anyhow. They're sort of a Boca thing.)

Must have been three or four hundred folks buying into old Steve's deal. Just about everybody in town can give you some version or so of the sales pitch and what was going on. Didn't even need a boiler-room operation, this time—just passed the word around down at the old barbershop.

Anyhow, it finally caught up with Steve, as hundreds of investors wanted to know more about the return on their money, and the local courts, some lawyers, and some judges got involved.

But young Steve might be back in bin-ness these days. Not necessarily at the same old stand, but happily bopping along, exploring new ideas—and maybe even some new investment plans for the world of tomorrow in Winter Haven.

Anyway, some good Winter Haven folks learned Grandaddy's Rule #9 that said, Experience is what helps you recognize your mistakes—when you make them again.

11

To Scam or Not to Scam; or, Money Can't Buy Happiness, but Happiness Can't Buy Groceries

IT MIGHT BE GOOD, at this point, to check on our progress so far on our journey through Scam Land. Let's see, we've visited with the fabled Prince Michael of Austria; we've toured grand old Boca Raton and a few of its stories; we've gone back to the Mizner land boom; and we've seen Florida's infamous railroad land giveaways back in the 1850s.

We've covered a lot of Florida's unique scams, and there are still many more to come up ahead. We've hardly gotten out of south Florida so far; it's time we got a move on. Now we're going explore some very personal, one-on-one scams. Maybe just one good old boy doing his thing, instead of these massive scams we've been learning about.

Human nature scams are the ones where that old devil, greed, takes over our otherwise down-to-earth, old-fashioned ethics. Stick around, it'll be interesting. Sometimes hard to believe, but interesting. So let's just pick a category at random.

How about education—we could start off around about 1900 to 1905, when the University of Florida sort of got spirited away from tiny Lake City down to Gainesville. (Some old-timers still wonder how that got accomplished.)

Or we could jump ahead nearly a century to an athletic director who was overseeing the department that produced the nation's number one college football team: now *there's* a case for you. This fellow was being paid $135,000 per year, plus an $11,000 annual annuity *and* a $12,000 yearly housing allowance. And still, the fellow somehow managed to get a free roofing job on his house from the guys that were over there working on the stadium. He got a $10,000 roof job for *free!* Virtually every newspaper, sports editor, and radio and TV reporter in the state picked it up.

After the investigation exploded and the media furor subsided a little bit, the fellow coughed up a $4,000 payment for that alleged $10,000 roofing job that the school had been charged for. He said it had just been an oversight. When the dust finally settled, the school *paid* the guy $300,000 to leave! I guess since it only cost the scammees (taxpayers) about a third of a million dollars, they got off lucky.

Remember Grandaddy's Rule #7—the one about man not eating his own kind, and so forth.

Now for the good news—there *is* a solution to all this carrying on. It's painfully simple and we'll get to it directly, right at the end of this chapter.

This next good old boy makes that first fellow seem like a rank beginner.

It's just a short hop over to Palm Beach County's incredible school board morass, which lasted over several years and several careers.

These words are in no way meant to be judgmental or accusatory, as the mess is slowly being cleaned up even at this writing. It is an area where the then school superintendent, as she took over her job in 1991, was described by attorney Don Feldman as having "inherited an orgy of incompetence, built on a black hole of golf, dinners, and other wondrous gifts from vendors." Not bad for openers.

You see, there was this big school board executive fellow—as our favorite wordsmith, John Grogan of the *Palm Beach Post,* said, "owner of perhaps the greasiest palm in the

Palm Beaches; he never met a favor he didn't like." Grogan called him the "Teflon Man." He said that he accepted all kinds of favors and gifts from suppliers who hoped to win big, juicy contracts supplying the school system with all kinds of good stuff. He went on Caribbean fishing trips on private yachts, spent weekends at mountain retreats, went on all-expense-paid golf outings, and attended lavish dinner parties (including one in Las Vegas that featured backrubs by toga-clad lovelies as part of the evening's entertainment). (I told you this guy was big-league.)

Now here comes the fast-shuffle, hard-to-believe part, so watch closely. As Yogi Berra used to say, "Listen very slowly."

Naturally, we assume the existence of an incredible sleuthing job . . . teams of gumshoes digging through dark, musty files to try to uncover tiny shreds of evidence leading to all of the above. Right?

Sorry, bunky. Wrong.

This fellow was so gentle, so simple in the ways of the world, that he carefully documented every single gift, every trip, every backrub in his own handwriting, using gushy thank-you notes which he sent to every supplier after virtually every goodie he received. In one letter, he wrote, "the food and wine were great, but the backrub was the best. It compared to my friendship with you." Boy howdy! So once the taxpayers had coughed up about a quarter of a million smackeroos in legal fees, they fired him.

And *then,* some new fellow comes along and says that the executive was wrongly treated. He says he was a wonderful guy and was just doing his job all along by going on all those fishing trips and toga parties and all. (It was dirty work but *somebody* had to do it.) And *then,* this second fellow says that the school board should reinstate the first fellow in good standing on all counts, and give him some $300,000 in back pay and legal bills.

So what happened to the good old boy? Well, they took him back, gave him a pay cut, and "demoted" him from purchasing stuff to being a school *principal*—at about $60-$80,000 a year! (Don't know about that back pay, though.)

And so the Parade of Purloining Personalities continues. We've only scratched the tip of the pyramid—(or was that supposed to be an iceberg?)—of Florida's dear old scams and scam artists . . . and even some of the scammees!

You know, some of these folks are just that: real artists. Some would bamboozle just a little handful of their friends and neighbors. Others might con a large gathering of investors out of their pocket change. And still others might hornswoggle a whole town, city, county, industry, or even a state or county education system, school board, or athletic department.

Now remember how I mentioned the solution? It's probably over-simplification, but one single word would go pretty far toward resolving such incredible messes. The word? It's *accountability*.

Citizens wanting to fight graft, cons, and scams should always look *behind* the "star" of the scam. Who—or what board—put the person in the job in the first place? What board created the job . . . and what board conducted the job search? Who handled the interviewing? What board designed and approved the employment contract? What group is keeping the person employed? To whom does the person report? How often? Who signs off on his or her work? And finally, who—if anybody—is watching the watchers?

It probably should have been one of Grandaddy's Rules.

The amazing part of the entire equation is that when you creep around behind the scenery, you find that, occasionally, *other* suave and debonair folks, smooth-talking jaspers, are *advising* the boards and committees on how to do their jobs. They tell them who to hire, how to design committees to do the watching, how to write those incredible golden-parachute employment contracts, and so on, ad infinitum.

Again, these pages do not try to be an indictment, or even a scolding. The courts take care of that. Everybody has a right to march to his or her own drummer. And like I said back on page two, or somewhere, the whole scam mentality—particularly when it comes to public monies—*has* to be a voluntary system. It all depends on you and me.

The object—the victim—of the scam simply has to be willing to go along with the scheme if the scam is going to work.

It all just seems to be a little easier when you're feeding at the billions of dollars floating around in the public trough.

Talking about those advisers, how about that $240-million computer system that the state folks say doesn't work right, but the company that sold it to them says that the state owes them about $12,000 a day *interest,* unless they (we) pay up. How come it takes two years of talks to *fail* to reach any agreement?

Or better yet, as my Associated Press friends and those folks at Taxwatch tell me, how about that extra million dollars that the Department of Education allocated to the Florida Association of District School Superintendents? That fund was for training programs to help boost the salaries of the elected and appointed top-level officials. And the association got almost *another* half-million to help pay their own dues to their own association. Taxwatch says that the funds will cover the dues of the association's sixty-seven members, of which forty-five are elected and twenty-two are appointed. (Hey, that's a *million and a half* of *your* dollars they're talking about.)

I reckon they must have some mighty good advisers telling them how to gitalong.

A scam is a scam, no matter how grand the stage or how majestic the players. And, except for these statewide plays, the scammee normally feels that he or she is about to get an extraordinarily good deal—maybe even that dream goal of something for nothing. Remember, this rule holds true—except when you're playing at the statewide level. There, the scammee—the taxpayer—is sometimes only going to get the nothing part. (See Grandaddy's Rule #1.)

And you may as well remember Rule #5 (the un-meek one) and Rule #7 (the skin 'em rule).

Heck, you may as well just remember them all. Because when it comes to your elected folks, especially their super advisers, there is a chance—just a chance—that the rules could probably all apply at one time or another.

At least that's what Grandaddy said.

12

Willie Popham the Oyster King and His Entire Empire

OH SURE, EVERYBODY KNOWS ABOUT Flagler and his Standard Oil millions, his railroads, and his hotels covering the Atlantic coast. And almost everybody has heard of Henry Plant of Plant City and *his* hotels and railroads. And maybe you've even heard about Chipley and his Panhandle rails, making him the "other railroader," or even S. Davies Warfield and his Seminole Inn at tiny Indiantown, and his dreams for Okeechobee as a giant city. (If you haven't heard of these guys, they're coming up soon.) And you've learned about the railroad barons and their six-mile-wide right-of-way for every mile of track they promised.

Wherever you travel in Florida, you find the names of these great men at almost every turn in the road. Names of the empire builders on towns, counties, buildings, parks, rivers, and bridges . . . on islands, streets, and boulevards.

Now, these men were not scam artists out to flimflam somebody out of their life savings. They didn't need to be.

They weren't hustling air-conditioning jobs, or furnace inspections, or aluminum siding. Nor were they trying to con folks out of a few bucks or even to sell them land.

They *were,* rather, master salesmen, visionaries, dreamers—and doers. Oh, with maybe just a few hustlers mixed in for good measure. They became a driving force in creating the new Florida and they enjoyed a lot of assistance from prospects in making it all happen.

And they became legend.

We have one of the most implausible, unlikely, surprising, and fascinating—and little-known—characters among all those legends coming right up.

This fellow represents a combination of traits and goodies almost too broad, too complex, too versatile, and therefore, too good to be true.

Now let's take all the *good* traits of an imaginary scam artist and combine them with all the attributes of the wonder-salesman profiled above, then stir in an amazing gift for inspirational pedagogy, actually from the pulpit . . . (wait—there's *more!)* . . . add a knack for writing popular novels of his time . . . along with the skill of poetry! . . . *plus* (still more) a natural bent for politics . . . and a grand talent in the business world as well. (Is there no end to this fellow?)

Would all this qualify the fellow as our true grand champion "super scammer" of all time?

Well, I should certainly *hope* so!

If we made him a schemer with the ability to attract investors into one giant venture after another, even *after* serving a jail sentence for fraud, would *that* help him to qualify? And then, how about if we rolled all these goodies together into a charming, friendly Sunday School superintendent? And *then,* how about if we made him mayor of the town—would that do it?

If you did all of the above, you'd eventually, irresistibly, and irrevocably wind up with William Lee Popham, the Oyster King of old Appalachicola, Franklin County, and Saint George Island.

Never heard of Popham? That's not too surprising. Check this out.

No photos of the man even exist in Joan Morris's Florida State million-print historical photo archives. And as historian Dr. William Warren Rogers points out, the entire Florida literature archive contains but a single copy of one of Popham's hundreds of direct-mail pamphlets, fliers, and brochures with their singing prose. In truth, the man practically *invented* direct-mail advertising with mail-outs which once virtually blanketed the southern and eastern United States. His brochures trumpeted his incredible ventures and adventures to unsuspecting potential investors. (Make a note of that mail technique. It'll come up again a little later on.)

He was really quite a guy.

As Rogers says, "What a character he was. Charismatic . . . confident . . . transfixing an audience with as oily a tongue as ever formed a word. . . .

"Charlatan, poet, evangelist, huckster, visionary . . . all these things . . . certainly one of the biggest fish ever to splash in a small Florida pond."

If you had been anywhere around Appalachicola from about 1916 on, then you'd know about Popham for sure. And you'd meet him again in Dr. Rogers's book, *Outposts on the Gulf.* Bill Rogers's works are always fascinating; we'll find no more riveting story than that of William Lee Popham, Esq.

The persona, exploits, and amazing accomplishments of the man simply know no equal. To grasp the dimensions of his twenty-year career, we're going to have to go chronologically.

By age seventeen (!), he was already honing his public speaking skills on the famed National Chatauqua Circuit, which hosted such giants as William Jennings Bryan.

By age twenty-one, he had already established a name for himself as a lecturer, evangelist, preacher, and spellbinder. He worked with titles such as "Men and Swine; Women and Wine." Wow! That was probably pretty heady stuff for the Chatauqua ticket-buyers in 1910.

At the same time, his first book, *The Road to Success: The Best Book in the World,* was already in the marketplace.

(Sounds like the Mizners used some of Popham's prose in the early advertising for their Boca Raton Land Company ads.)

By 1911, he had more than a dozen published pieces, from poetry to his saccharine romantic novels featuring heroines named LaVerne Sunbeam, Dixie Darlington, and Daisy Sunflower!

Hey, old Popham was fixing to start to really move the merchandise. And he was all of about twenty-three years old by this time.

1912: On his honeymoon trip to Tampa, he decides to settle there. (Probably thinks he might buy the place.) He becomes a citrus grower, using funds from his lectures, revival meetings, and book sales. He thinks he might retire and write. After all, by now, he's pushing twenty-four.

1916: He runs unsuccessfully for Hillsborough County Commission. Upon losing the election, he decides to visit the Panhandle. He falls in love with Saint George Island and the region; he thinks he might buy *it.* And he does (now watch my hands at all times, folks), giving as down payment the copyrights to his poems, his first book, and a couple of his lectures. Hey, old Willie Popham, almost twenty-four, has finally found *Mr. Right!*

As Rogers points out, this very first deal would spawn many clones over the next twenty years.

Popham was becoming truly a man made for his time . . . and he was barely getting underway.

1916: He begins to develop his prose style. He lays out promotional schemes to develop his Saint George Island, and uses Popham trademark phrases like, "God's favored isle" and "a leisure time Utopia where sunbeams play like angels . . . by the dream-kissed Florida Sea." (By the way, that "Florida Sea" was probably the Gulf of Mexico, but we can't be too sure with Willie.)

Next, he tries to create a workers' commune on the island. He sends out thousands of fliers and brochures in the U.S. mail, which he has recently discovered. His brochures, also dripping with that good old "Popham Syrup" that he used in his novels and poems, were preaching virtues of "shared play and work in paradise . . . where colonists would fish, hunt, and woo to the sweet song of the sad sea." Boy howdy! This fellow is talking to some good old cracker farmers about *wooing!* I mean, that might get those old cracker farmers wound up tighter than Dick's hatband! But boy, could he *sell!*

One of Willie's main business ventures for the island colonists to work in—when they're not busy wooing, we may assume—is—are you ready?—the farming of porpoises! His press releases, brochures, and investment solicitations tell of how the sea mammals would be trapped and butchered, you know, like they did with hogs.

Popham goes on to say that, after a single tantalizing taste, the poignant (?) flavor of porpoise meat would sweep the country, becoming an instant hit with seafood lovers everywhere! (Wait. There's more.)

As a special bonus, he plans giant factories to tan the porpoise hides and manufacture the finest shoelaces in the world.

He also farms oyster-beds, which becomes a major area seafood industry. Popham's mail-outs become mollusk magnets, drawing investors to his Oyster Empire.

It is truly destined to become a workers' paradise.

Now at this point, Florida is creeping toward her incredible land boom. And *this* proved to be a stage made for a William Lee Popham, Esq., if ever there was one.

Popham, through his mailers, now planned to turn Saint George Island into a tropical vacationers' mecca. But he was getting on in years—must have been about twenty-seven or twenty-eight by now.

Anyhow, investors begin to pour in, bringing their money.

1918-1920: Postwar investors arrive daily. They're responding to Popham's fantastic mail overtures, all seeking to tap into the Popham Oyster Empire on the "fairy-kissed island." They are probably serenaded at the dock by Dixie, LaVerne, and Daisy, who, by now, have formed a singing group and are looking for a record contract.

1920 (estimated): Popham, seeing hundreds of speculators storming the bastions of his dream world, kicks off his "Million-Dollar Bond Plan" (through that U.S. mail, again). He plans to take a little ten-room inn on the island and build a *thousand-room hotel,* complete with multi-colored seashell walls. He announces the plan in his own newspaper, *The Oyster Farm News* (what else?).

1922 (estimated) He becomes president of the Chamber of Commerce.

1924 (estimated): He is elected mayor of the town. The world is his—you guessed it.

1925: Postal authorities (whoops!) suddenly find Popham and his wife guilty of mail fraud, and of apparently "leasing oyster bottoms to out-of-state folks." (I didn't know they could get you for that. He probably got crossways with some of the good old boys down at the courthouse—they'll get you every time.)

Four years of legal battles end up with Popham serving two years in Atlanta's Federal Penitentiary, then returning to Appalachicola where he is greeted by a large crowd of dockside fans. (And possibly serenaded by Dixie, LaVerne, and Daisy.)

1928: Popham is right back on top again. He forms companies to market seafood in *powdered, cubed, and tablet form.* He also plans a chain of three thousand Oyster Huts, coast-to-coast—probably going to have Oyster McNuggets for breakfast. Folks will line up to buy the stuff!

1928-1930: He decides to market a new soft drink at his proposed three thousand Oyster Huts. The stuff is going to be called—ready?—Oyster Nip! No, seriously, folks. "Both nutritious and delicious! And good for you, too, kids! Just five cents a glass! Drink it hot or cold!"

1930s somewhere: He launches Florida Sunland Farms, a new idea to sell five-acre farms for only $60 each—by mail—to poor, depression-stricken northerners, of which there are millions, for their place in the sun.

The land boom has now slithered to a halt, wallowing around in the Great Depression, and is dying a lingering death, so Popham was now about ten years *behind* his times.

1930s: Following Sunland, he plans "The Florida Goat, Sheep, and Turkey Farms." (I'm not sure whether they were to be all at the same time, or each as a separate venture. The corporate papers begin to get blurred about this time.) But anyhow, all of it was to be based on his Saint George Island. This venture turns the island into a giant ranch, with Daisy, Dixie, and LaVerne singing that famous old classical/western song, "They're Rustlin' in the Old Bach Chorale."

The man simply exploded with ideas.

And then, guess what?

1936: He *again* faced federal indictment for mail fraud! This time it involved gold and silver mines in Texas. Attaboy! He faces his *second* trial and sentencing.

In his trial, *Popham defends himself!* He talks as smoothly and effectively as he writes. He summons thirty-five years of oratory, prose, preaching, poetry, and writing . . . and simply mesmerizes the jury, which promptly acquits him of all charges.

You just have to love the guy.

Well sir, Popham finally leaves his Appalachicola center stage in 1938, penniless and broken-spirited. You see, the guys with the gift of scamming money usually can't stop spending it. And most of it wasn't even really there, anyway.

Willie worked his way to Los Angeles, where he completed his life in 1953.

His last job was working as a real estate salesman.

In Frank Stephenson's excellent review of Rogers's book, many avenues were explored trying to sum up in a few lines the drive—the incredible spark and fire—that drove that man for three decades. Each avenue that was tried proved that it simply couldn't be done.

Some local folks say he was the victim of jealous business competitors, who simply didn't want to let Popham succeed with all of his amazing dreams.

Others agree that he really did believe in himself—and in all of his dreams. Was he a shyster? Possibly. But as Stephenson says, he was probably a far greater force for good than for evil.

Hustler? Promoter? Visionary? Good con man? Absolutely—he was all of these; but he was also much more.

From the time in 1924 when his companies were bringing in some $24,000 *every day,* to his plans to make the world's finest shoestrings out of porpoise hides, the man who planned to make Franklin County the Satsuma Capital of the World was, as Rogers put it, an absolute pro at knowing how to dance a long, long time on somebody else's dime.

But Rogers and Stephenson also agree that Popham, the master of them all—even when you *knew* you were being hustled and hosed, and *he* knew that *you* knew he was putting something over on you—he still genuinely *liked* you.

And somehow, you knew that, too.

13

Why Are People Like Ostriches?; or, If You Stick Your Head in the Sand, You'll Never See It Coming

ONE GOOD THING ABOUT OLD POPHAM and his Oyster Empire with his porpoise shoelaces and his Oyster Nip beverage was that Popham's gigantic scams started back around 1919 or so.

Things were different then; life was a whole lot simpler. Folks could be sold something like porpoise-hide shoelaces a lot easier then than in modern times. They would also flock to pay ten cents just to look at a big, sleepy snake, or to see Wilson Mizner and his dancing bear—or even to look at a new Model T that just came to town.

Why, folks today would never go for such a dumb scam. We're a whole lot more sophisticated. We read, listen to the radio, watch TV, and really study our investments carefully!

Right!

Oyster Nip? Pshaw; it would never happen today.

Oh yes, there was just *one* similar scam that came along that was almost as wild and woolly as Popham's Oyster Empire.

How about *the ostrich!* Now *there's* a great investment for you. The meat would sell as health food; the hides could be used for something, I suppose; and everybody knows about the famous ostrich feather—*that* could become a rare collector's item. Say! We could develop chains of ostrich-breeding farms.

Why, I'll bet we could produce *thousands* of the big birds. Yeah! We could sell the feathers, market the meat, empty out the eggs and sell the eggshells to artists. Hey, then we could even franchise the whole shebang to investors worldwide! What an idea! What a deal! We could even go public and sell the stock over the telephone!

Yes sir, it's a pure 1920s scam if I ever saw one.

What's that you say? It was year before last? Awww, come on now. Nobody would bite on ostrich ranches clear up here in the 1990s.

Well, welcome to the twentieth century, and the giant ostrich egg and ostrich ranch scam! And Fred Schulte knows the whole story.

Fred Schulte, the investigations editor for the *Sun-Sentinel* in Fort Lauderdale, is an interesting guy—if you like major-league investigative editors who go around winning all kinds of national awards for giant exposés and stuff like that.

Fred's digging covers fraud, scams, rip-offs, and cons of all kinds; one of his specialties is telemarketing scams. In his book, *Fleeced!,* Schulte deals principally with those telemarketing scams and how to handle phone rip-off artists. One of Fred's great lines in the book—which almost sums up the entire phone-scam industry—is his famous advice to young cub reporters: "Remember, if your mother says she loves you, check it out."

It was in this book that Fred brought us the story of ostrich eggs: America's next great cash crop!

It actually happened in the early 1990s, when one of those smooth-talking bunches of boiler-room guys began hustling shares in ostrich-breeding farms.

Nobody seems too sure of just how it actually took off. There was a lot of press about ostriches at the time, about how they had fancy feathers, durable hides, low-calorie meat, breeding potential, artsy ostrich eggs . . . and the first thing you know, Florida boiler rooms were hustling investment shares in ostrich-breeding farms.

One guy told Fred, "It's easy to take something that's legitimate and run a scam . . . you just play on people's greed. If you tell a good enough story, folks will just send you their money."

The phoners touched over a thousand buyers in forty-eight states for more than $3 million to invest in one big "ostrich ranch" somewhere in south Florida.

And in this case, they were promising returns of *40 to 60 percent interest on your money within the first year.*

(At this point, those little alarm bells should have begun going off like crazy, and the smart folks would have looked up Grandaddy's Rule #1.)

The "think tank" ostrich experts had this one all figured out, down to the last egg: they knew how many chicks would be born each season; how many eggs they would sell; and an "estimated seasonal profit." Heck, at one time, they were so confident of their project, they were even offering prospects a money-back guarantee. (They may have gotten off that wagon pretty quick, hy-ever.)

The scam seemed to have everything. The phoners were actually selling general partnerships in the venture, so buyers felt that they would be helping to run the company. What could be a surer thing than that?

As it turned out, most of the folks really didn't know what a general partnership was, but it sounded real good. As a matter of fact, the first plan sold so well, promoters immediately opened a second phase . . . it was all almost too good to be true! (And that's where Grandaddy's Rule #6 should have kicked in: If it sounds too good to be true, it probably is.)

Anyway, apparently, no record could be found of anybody ever making a single dime in profits from the ostrich eggs or ostrich ranches—or whatever—except, of course, the promoters. And it was about this time that the company's wheels began to fall off.

A lot of investors began to learn for the very first time

that "general partners" can be held liable for the entire sum of a company's debts, liabilities, and obligations, if the other "general partners" can't pay their share.

They also learned—late in the game—that one of the main promoters had a list of altercations with securities lawmen all over the place: felony charges in Texas; selling unregistered securities all over; franchising "teen discos" in some other towns; and selling "vacation certificates." It turned out that the fellow was a master of the 900-number system of working the marketplace.

In this last deal, he even had automatic phone-dialers and taped voices ringing up millions of phone numbers. (You haven't lived until you start talking to a voice and discover that it's a machine.) The dialers would tell folks that they had won a free vacation trip, but would have to send some money to pay for incidentals—maybe shipping and handling and stuff like that.

This fellow had just about done them all.

Folks said probably his biggest deal had been selling some oil and gas well deals out of his old Florida boiler rooms—until he found out about the ostrich!

Papa Johnson would have loved the ostrich, too—it was his kind of deal.

14

The Gulf American Land Saga

FLORIDA'S LAND HAS BEEN A SOURCE of scams throughout her history.

This has been true from the days of the earliest promoters, all the way back to the Marquis de LaFayette, when a grateful fledgling nation gave the Marquis some two hundred thousand acres of land, anywhere on the continent he wished . . . and he chose Florida. The Marquis never saw his gift. He never visited his land, but rather handed it over to agents who—it is said—immediately put it up for sale to other promoters.

From this beginning, through those Internal Improvements Commission fellows I told you about with their ultra-fun railroad games, it was but a small step to the previously-mentioned 1920s land boom and the innovative ploy of selling land by the gallon.

Now remember, the Internal Improvements Commission back in the early 1850s was where railroad presidents served on the government board, awarding land grant bonuses to themselves. These gifts of land, in many cases, were simply handed off to promoters to be sold to the public. The railroad guys were apparently reading the Marquis de LaFayette handbook.

This easygoing, good old boy system of government

worked so well in nearly every nook and cranny of 1850s Florida that it easily carried over into the 1920s.

Here, tracts of land changed hands four, five, six—even eight times in a single day. It was sort of a gigantic, fifty-eight-thousand-square-mile crapshoot in which there were always some winners and some losers. Florida found hundreds of major-league players converging on their own, personal, larger than life game board to play the Florida Land Game.

All this carried over into the post-World War II period. Ahhh, the '50s.

You see, there were approximately four million GIs stationed in Florida during the war. After the war, they left, and then most of them began to pour *back* into the Land of Sunshine. This time they brought their young wives and little kids to build a new life for themselves . . . and a new Florida for all.

Suddenly, population soared. The numbers reflected the incoming traffic, from about one million in 1940 to two million in 1950, from four million in 1960 to nearly eight million in the 1970s, and approaching fifteen million in the 1990s.

It was during the 1950s that one of the very first of the true behemoth land promotion companies began to take shape in the vision of two fellows from up Baltimore way.

These two bright young go-getters, Leonard and Jack Rosen, certainly knew a golden opportunity when it hit them in the face, and they took action.

David Dodrill does a superb job of documenting the Rosens and their fantastic moves in his book, *Selling the Dream; the Gulf American Corporation and the Building of Cape Coral, Florida.* And my old friend, historian and author Stuart McIver, does an equally fine job in reviewing Dodrill's book in *The South Florida History Magazine.*

In his book, Dodrill states that the beginning of Gulf American was when the Rosens acquired some seventeen hundred acres of land at Redfish Point near Fort Myers in 1957. They eventually created the largest land sales company in the whole nation. Its sales skyrocketed to $124 million by 1966, a greater amount than the next *four* Florida land sales companies combined, only to have the rocket begin to plummet by 1969.

Dodrill's account also relates firsthand stories of the sales techniques used by the hard sellers in these land promotion companies. With regard to high-pressure sales tactics (which do not, of themselves, constitute a scam of any kind), one marketing executive with the company said, "We built a company on street fighters."

One former salesman recalled, "At first we sold Cape Coral as a legitimate community . . . then Golden Gate Estates with roads and not much else . . . then River Ranch with nothing at all . . . and finally Remuda Ranch with lots that were still under water. Everything worked."

He later added, "One of the bosses said that eventually, we'll just mail out contracts and folks will send them back with their checks and we'll tell them where we're going to put them." Only difference from the '20s land boom hustlers was that *they* had to jump on your car's running boards and stick the contracts through your window!

Overpriced lots were sold as "investments," when the company knew that there was no resale market whatsoever. Many customers would buy multiple lots to "hold for rising prices."

As Dodrill's narrative reports, occasionally lots were even switched around without informing the buyers. At the same time, the company was enlisting sales agents all over the midwest who were selling lots to local customers for only $30 down and $30 per month. If the buyers had checked Grandaddy's Rule #14, they would have learned Grandaddy's Old Cracker Payment Plan: Everything down and nothing a month for the rest of your life.

Anyway, it all worked out just fine. In the midwestern

sales offices, thousands of tiny little lots were outlined on a huge wall-sized map hanging in the real estate fellow's lobby. You could just stand there and study those thousands of little tiny lots, and imagine your new life in sunny Florida. It created an especially hypnotic effect on a ten-above-zero, dark, gray, snowy, sleety February afternoon.

And boy, they had color brochures and everything. The downtown offices would even have color slides for you to look at. Then they had a real simple form for you to sign, and whammo! You were a real live Florida landowner.

For the tiny little lots, the amount was so modest, you didn't even mind that you were buying from a blown-up picture—of an artist's rendering—of a sketch—of a plot plan—of a blueprint.

The rendering was of a beautiful Florida waterfront community, with every one of those five thousand little lots numbered for easy reference. You and the missus could stand there and discuss, "Well I like #2314, over here, it's on this little canal and it's going to overlook this little bay . . ."

You were transported in the theatre of the mind.

It looked like almost every little house was going to be located on some kind of beautiful canal or waterway or gorgeous bay of some kind.

As a matter of fact, it even seemed like every little house had a thirty-seven-foot cruiser parked in the backyard. Some of the little folk probably thought the boat came with the lot—and all for only $30 a month. (Most of them never stopped to figure out how long it would take to pay for all this at $30 a month.)

Sometimes salesmen would take prospects up in small planes and point out a specific lot being carefully worked on. "Hey, Fred and Evelyn, I think that's your lot, right down there. Looks great, doesn't it?" Except that they only had one lot being worked on and they showed the same lot to every new prospect they closed.

There are known instances of families who, forty years

later, are still trying to *find* the pair of lots that Grandma bought.

The unraveling of the Gulf American promotions, along with General Development and other similar giant Florida land promotion firms, was so complex that it consumes three hundred pages of Dodrill's book. Suffice it to say that excesses in Florida land sales were measurable enough to call for the establishment of the Florida Installment Land Sales Board, which would oversee all such developments for the next generation.

Chances are, those land scams were creatures of their time that will never live again. So we can all relax, let down our guard, and not bother with silly details like reading sales contracts—even the small print. And we can be secure in the knowledge that nobody would ever dream of trying to take advantage of us in some kind of deal.

And just as soon as we do, someday, somewhere, some smiling good old boy is going to sidle up to us and say, "Friend, if you'll buy that, I've got some land in the Everglades I want to talk to you about." That's Grandaddy's Rule #11. And suddenly, it'll be the 1920s—or the 1950s—all over again. And there's just not that much cider to go around.

15

If You're a Senior, You're a Target

THE LIST OF SCAMS JUST KEEPS on growing, with no apparent end in sight. With each passing day, new stories surface. There's a scam to meet every need.

Let's just wander around the house for a moment . . . say! How about that old air-conditioner? How's it doing? It's pretty old hat, I'd say. We can have a new one delivered right from our truck outside in minutes. The truck is right down the street. Of course, we need a small deposit. You can understand that. There we go. Now we'll take the deposit, go call in the order from the truck . . . and *be right back.*

Now there are several major clues in that exchange; the most prominent one is "leaving" (especially "leaving with your deposit").

No matter what the approach, it's all often a variation of the old siding game from back up north in Chicago, or Detroit, or Youngstown, or Milwaukee, or wherever.

In one case, the little old lady was called on the phone by a charming gentleman who sounded so very mature and distinguished. He offered her a very special—almost free—air conditioning inspection, right there in her own home—almost for nothing!

Now at those last two words alone, that little warning buzzer should have gone off in her ear. And if she'd had her list of Grandaddy's Rules handy, right there by the phone, she'd have instantly looked up Rule #1 and saved herself a whole peck of grief.

When the "inspectors" got there, they immediately pointed out a "leak" in an obscure part of her air-conditioner. The seventy-four-year-old lady, alarmed by warnings from the inspectors (who seemed like such nice young men), reluctantly agreed to a new $3,000 unit.

It was a tiny consolation to the lady to learn that more than four hundred seniors just like her were also conned in this air-conditioning scam in south Florida.

The Florida Department of Law Enforcement says that many scams of this type seem to concentrate solely on the folks between the ages of sixty-five and ninety-five.

In one severe case, two senior ladies were taken for some $50,000—over an extended period of time—in unnecessary repairs and maintenance on their home heating and air-conditioning systems.

The scammers prey on the seniors because they are always on the lookout for a "laydown," a victim who can be easily bamboozled, even by beginner scammers.

The expert scammer will often utilize speed as an ally. In almost every case, the elderly are urged "act *now!*" . . . "don't put this off" . . . "make the deposit today! You can always ask for it back if you change your mind!"

All this calls for Grandaddy's Rule #10, which urged: If you're going to go wrong, go slow. You won't have to back up far to clean up your mess.

The air-conditioning scam grew so big that it drew national attention. It was determined that it was going on all over the country, wherever seniors tended to congregate. National seniors' organizations urged their members to be on the alert for any such approaches.

Now scanning our scam menu, punch up *P.* Just about everybody has heard—at one time or another—about the famed "pigeon-drop" operation. It is a simple one, and it's simply amazing how often it still works . . . and how easily. I mentioned it briefly a while back.

This is the basic maneuver where the fellow in the bus station (or post office, or mall parking lot, you name it) tells you that he has just found a bag containing $5,000. And he is so overjoyed at his good fortune, he wants to share it with someone. And you look like such a nice person, and he's sure you would do the same thing for him if *you* had found the five thou in a paper bag, so he's chosen you to share it with.

Now he feels that you both should put up some kind of good-faith deposit. (That means money.) So you both put up a deposit. This probably will consist of however much loose cash you have on your body at the time.

Now comes the tricky part. Scam trainees practice for years to learn to master this maneuver. He has to go to the bathroom and will be right back. (Refer to "leaving" again.)

The scammer never returns. The scammee is left with nothing . . . nada . . . zero . . . zip and zilch. Except maybe a lightened sensation in the pocketbook and a valuable lesson. (This one is a variation on that old Hank Thompson Instant Teaching Machine I told you about.)

There's a variation on the old pigeon drop that can be even more damaging. This is the one where the nice young men have the "mark" sign several very handsome and impressive forms which call for a small deposit. (The deposit is fully refundable, of course, under the absolute, money-back warranty, if you're not fully satisfied.) One of my advisers tells me that "warranty" nowadays often seems to be a more attractive word to the mark than "guarantee." No one appears to know exactly why.

The nice young men then reluctantly accept the deposit, which is maybe only a couple hundred dollars, and graciously leave, saying they'll be back first thing in the morning with the "installation crew." This brings up "leaving" again. Avoid this move.

The solution to falling for these scams? This one's easy. It's Grandaddy's Rule #15: You always do bin-ness with your kinfolk. (And knowing both grandaddies, I expect they were fairly careful with some of the kinfolk, too.) This keeps you safe from charming strangers.

But chances are you won't have that many kinfolk hanging around in modern times, so you'll do well just to check with trusted advisers before signing any papers or making any major purchases. And read the small print!

16

Danny and the Inmates Dupe the IRS

THIS ONE IS *REALLY* HARD TO BELIEVE. The fellows in this case should have been paying attention to Grandaddy's Rule #8 (the large print giveth and the small print taketh away). Here's how it worked.

There was this fellow, see, down in Fort Lauderdale. He was hired by some dudes to do them a small, simple favor. All he had to do was just take some checks down to the bank, cash them, and bring the money back to the office to collect his pay, which was going to be—ready?—*one thousand dollars.* Not too bad for a simple check-cashing errand. The banks seemed to cash the checks okay, so no problem.

It turned out that the checks were from the IRS. And they were refund checks. That's right. They were IRS refund checks (plural). Said so right there in great big letters. (This is the part where they should have read the large print—especially those particular *three big letters.)*

Anyhow, it turned out that the IRS tax refund checks were based on *fictitious* tax returns. So the plot thickens. These fictitious tax returns all called for tax refunds. And these tax refunds were paid to nonexistent taxpayers. Now we're getting someplace. Even if you're not paying close attention, you can probably tell something's coming up right smart and shortly, too.

Anyway, these geeks even had a corporate business plan. They had projections, pro formas, and all that good stuff. Maybe they even had some consultants in the neighborhood to help them draw them up. (We'll get to their neighborhood in just a moment.)

As they say in the wonderful world of economist-consultant buzzword jargon, their near-term goal was simple. It was to skim about $800,000 from the IRS—not bad for openers.

Their plan was to be promulgated (another great economist-consultant word) over a period of forty-eight months.

Now bubba, it don't take no rocket scientist to figure all that out, does it? They were going to use those clever, fictitious IRS income tax returns from some nonexistent people to receive some very *real* tax-refund dollars from the IRS when this good old boy cashed those checks. No wonder they paid the guy a thou for the job.

So you've got it all figured out, so far. It's a simple tax check scam. But wait—there's more. And here comes the juicy, hard-to-believe part.

This plan was conceived by a couple of guys over at the Glades Correctional Institution in Belle Glade. I mean they were *inside* the tank. That's right. The whole shillelagh was put together, with chewing gum, orange crates, and bailing wire, by a couple of prisoners at Glades.

They used names and social security numbers of some fellow inmates and filed tax returns claiming tax refunds. They then smuggled the forms outside the walls to another guy, who hired the third guy to go cash the checks when they came in.

Of course you and I know it's far too silly and too complicated and farfetched ever to work. And besides, who'd want to tangle with the IRS in a scam, anyway. Right?

Wrong. These guys collected about $70,000 from IRS refund checks over their first two seasons before they were discovered and shut down.

And here we thought we'd seen them all. Just remember Grandaddy's Rule #5, about the un-meek.

17

The Real Great Adventures of Mindy and Jeff and the Let's Pretend Airline

FLORIDA HAS THEM ALL—SCAMS that are grand and scams that are small. Way up there near the top rungs of the ladder, we often find the more complex, unique, and astonishing scams, which require pure genius.

How about the guy who successfully skimmed (pluperfect post-subjunctive mode of the rambunctious infinitive "to scam") about *eight hundred grand* from an imaginary airline! That's right—his *imaginary* airline.

I guess what it was, was, he sort of skimmed the $800,000 from the people he said he was going to train to fly his make-believe airplanes in his Let's Pretend Airline. Nobody seemed to know anything for sure by the time it got to a certain point.

For this one, we have to take you back to old Boca Raton again. (Sorry about that, but that's where the action is.)

Now see, the fellow who had his airline . . . no wait . . . he never really *said* he had an airline . . . no wait, yes . . . he did say he had an airline . . . at least once or twice I think he said it.

Maybe he said he was *going to* have an airline. Yes, I'm sure that's it. He was going to plan to have an airline once he got everything all straightened out and could get to it.

So there's this guy, see. Very suave, good-looking dude in his early thirties, with super-good-looking suits and whole bunches of exotic cars to ride around in. Heck, investigators found that this fellow was leasing *eleven* exotic cars for his company. He had a Lotus, a Bentley, a 'Vette, *and* a Jag to tool around in.

Boy howdy! He just didn't mess around. Did I mention that he only wore handmade custom *eye*-talian shoes? Well, that's what some folks said. And that's probably where some of that $60,000 credit card bill came in. Carrying cash can be so tacky, you know.

Oh by the way, that $60,000 worth of credit-card charges was *just for one month!* Now how do you suppose you could rack up sixty grand in credit-card charges in just one month? You'd have to be working at it twenty-four hours a day. But this young man got it done! And you'll have to agree, that's real motivation.

Well anyway, this fellow with the Let's Pretend Airline and the credit-card charges seemed to have all the right parts in all the right places.

Apparently, he planned to sell some sort of shares in his dream airline to the people he was hiring to work for the company. So far so good. No problem with that, right? So the pilots he was hiring were being charged $5,000 to come in and the flight attendants were being charged $2,000, and all the money was supposed to earn dividends and all, once they got the thing rolling . . . errr, flying.

First thing you know, some old nosy-parker said whoa! You guys are selling unregistered securities without a license. At this point, the company said oh no . . . this money is for the training costs of the pilots and attendants. You SEC guys got us all wrong.

Like we said, the dapper young man really appeared to have it all together. He had his dream airline on the drawing boards. He had his eleven cars—or whatever. His folks were hiring pilots and flight attendants left and right, and collecting those fees for "training costs," up to around $800,000 or so.

Anyway, he had it all together, until he finally stumbled across a major problem. Her name was Mindy Brockman. (Actually, he encountered a whole bunch of these problems, pilot Jeff Margolf among them, but Mindy turned out to be a *major,* major problem.)

Now Mindy is a lady who doesn't appreciate being taken to the cleaners. When she and a friend heard about the new luxury airline-to-be, they applied for jobs as flight attendants. But when Mindy learned that the airline was charging attendants $2,000 and pilots $5,000 for what were called training fees, she drew on her previous experience as a legal secretary with big corporations up north and began asking some simple questions.

Mindy says she noted an instant withdrawal from her questions—a cool response—from the company folk she was querying, and she immediately knew two things: (*a*) that she probably would not be hired, and (*b*) that this deal was probably too good to be true.

Mindy had somehow instinctively learned Grandaddy's Rule #6: If it sounds too good to be true, it probably is.

Mindy Brockman found herself leading a team of ten helpers, working a telephone network, and sending out more than one hundred newsletters contacting potential victims of the now-famous airline training scam. The case drew the attention of the Florida State Attorney's office, the Florida Department of Law Enforcement, the SEC, the FAA, and possibly even the FBI.

By the time the dust had begun to settle, it had turned out that the airline tycoon had also been involved in some real estate fraud in Canada from 1985 to 1987, involving a couple million dollars. Apparently, some of the Canadian folk—at this writing—are still waiting to hear about *their* money.

The incredible part of the program, says Jeff Margolf, professional pilot and former military (and present reserve) flier, is that if the entire drill was really a scam, then the principals spent tons of money that they didn't need to. They placed nationwide advertising in *USA Today* to attract employees from all across the nation and South America; hired training crews to man the giant 747 aircraft; and even rented huge flight simulators which apparently were never going to be used.

As a professional pilot, Margolf can readily address such strange budget items as these, which may account for at least a little bit of *his* $5,000. As Jeff says, company officials said that they planned to hire more than 150 pilots, nearly 400 flight attendants, and more than 500 other staffers.

Let's see now, 150 pilots at $5,000 apiece is $750,000 . . . 400 flight attendants at $2,000 each is $800,000 . . . that's about $1.5 million so far. Now add some fees from those other 500 staff members . . . all this might at least go toward helping pay off some of that $60,000 credit-card bill . . . and maybe even those eleven leased cars.

But it would probably only pay the rental on that old 747 for about an hour and a half.

Maybe we could just charter it for company picnics and leave it on the ground. Be a lot cheaper that way.

At any rate, Mindy may find herself with an entirely new career as sort of a "Ms. Robin Hood for scammees." If so, she'll probably find no shortage of clients calling for her services.

And if somebody calls you about a job with a brand-new airline, ask about their company cars and check out the CEO's style of clothing—especially be on the lookout for those custom handmade *eye*-talian shoes.

Maybe you just better get acquainted with Mindy and keep her number handy. She might be a good person to know.

18

Florida: the Magic Land—Where Money Disappears

WHAT IS THIS MAGIC, THIS SCAM EUPHORIA that draws such a crowd of the easy-buck people to Florida? Dozens of pundits have written about the magnetic attraction. Countless barristers theorize daily in case after case on the fatal attraction that Florida has for the scammer.

Some cons are harmless enough, unless, of course, you happen to be the one getting conned.

This is very much akin to the famous old miracle diet that said you could eat anything you want—as long as you just don't swallow.

Better Business Bureaus all over Florida and the nation provide endless lists of complaints.

A direct-mail company operating from New York to almost all points in Florida sent out thousands of beautiful letters telling folks that they had won a free luxury car.

The letter then casually mentioned that the receiver had to forward a small good-faith deposit . . . about $50 to $100 . . . for "processing fees."

Remember when I told you about "leaving" ? Well, here is where we learn about "sending." Sending is equally undesirable, especially if it appears in a smooth-talking letter from a total stranger telling you that you've just won a *free car.* And even more especially if the letter is addressed, Dear

Occupant. (But I really shouldn't have to point that out, now should I?) Anyway, add "sending" to your Key Words List.

But a whole lot of folks *did* send in some money to that New York firm. And they quickly received—guess what—another letter asking them to send in some more money. You can see how "sending" can be just as clumsy and cloying as "leaving" is. Both are to be avoided.

This "free car" gambit doesn't eclipse the "phony invoice" mail technique used by some small-time operators. These simply have some printed forms developed which look just like a standard invoice for some service rendered to your medium-sized company. The amount in the pay column will always be modest.

Most operations will put a figure in the $37.82 to $64.90 range. An actual one-time operator (reformed) of this scam told me years ago that the number of times he would receive a regular corporate check for the amount shown was mind-boggling. A company clerk opening the mail would place the "invoice" in the to-be-paid folder, and many times the payment would simply go out in the mail for the imaginary service. To be carefully within the law, the inscription, "This is not an invoice" was carefully placed somewhere on the form. But it was often overlooked by the mail clerk.

It was a simple numbers game; the more "invoices" that were mailed out, the better the odds of receiving some checks. This scam does, however, require lots of change-of-address forms, since the billing firm must, of necessity, move about quite often.

Eventually it must clear out of town. This lead us to Papa Johnson's small Rule #13a: Don't never go into bin-ness with a fellow named Skip.

It also reminds us of Rule # 8 (read that small print!).

Lists of scams and frauds are developed, maintained, and expanded by Better Business Bureaus all over the land.

(Reminds me of the guy who called his Better Business Bureau to ask why business wasn't better . . .) Anyway, these bureaus remain your single most effective source for seeking information, action, and even consolation in knowing that you are not alone as a scam victim. The staffs should be commended for their continuous efforts on behalf of consumers.

Consumers who, many times, should have known better than to get involved with the scam in the first place.

Let's close this chapter with an anecdote about consumers who might be tempted to be scammers.

The machine people tell me that they're developing new machines that will catch you if you try to speed through the tollbooth on the turnpike without throwing your quarter in the basket! Somehow, this little machine will actually read your license plate, or something, as you speed away. It will then quickly alert its capitalist bosses to write you a nasty letter. The letter will say something like, Hey, we've got your number. Now send us your quarter.

Officials tell me that it's amazing how many people will actually send in their quarters when they're accosted by a scam-catcher machine that's smarter than they are . . . and when they're written to in that firm tone of voice (or tone of print).

By the way, from our free information department, for you compulsive toll skippers and tollbooth deadbeats, since you're just little beginner scammers, you may as well know that the lane nearest the tollbooth is the one you want to avoid. Only about 1 percent of the skippers try to make it through that lane. (High visibility and all, don't you know.) The far outside lanes—the ones farthest from the toll-taker's window—account for about 7 percent of the folks who sometimes try to scam the good old Florida D.O.T. out of its quarter.

19

The Monster Python and the Hustler Hall of Fame

I SUPPOSE WE COULD JUST HOLD a vote on the scam of the month award and probably never run out of the creative ideas that leap from the minds of truly gifted scam artists. As rapidly as one good scam becomes sort of old hat, some wise-talking jasper comes up with a new one, a new twist on an old one, or a new way of approaching the "laydown."

What continues to amaze analysts and real smart folks who study such stuff is that even the oldest trick, the most ancient dodge in the trade, will continue to find new marks. It seems that there are folks who will simply go out of their way to be conned.

And that's about all it takes.

We could go back to the un-bathed German nobleman, von Moser, in old Miami. (Early crackers, just like folks in I-oh-way, Indiana, or Illinois, seemed to have an affinity for de-frocked, deposed, de-throned nobility from the Old World . . . no matter what sort of snake oil they might be selling.)

Anyway, von Moser claimed to have captured the world's largest python, honest, right there in Brickell Hammock, just off Old Cutler Road, south of Miami's 1910 downtown.

The deposed German nobleman (probably a distant cousin of Prince Michael of Austria) rented an old garden shop and displayed the thing. Charged folks ten cents just to come and take a look at the lethargic behemoth. Literally hundreds of folks came to look—and pay their dimes.

Hey, it was 1910! And life may have been a bit less than a thrill-a-minute for the little people of the day. Maybe looking at a big snake was *worth* ten cents in 1910.

Well sir, an astute young newspaper reporter decided to check out von Moser's German nobleman background. The reporter found that nobody knew for sure if von Moser had ever even *been* to Germany.

The reporter also found out some interesting tidbits about Mr. Python. He was supposed to have been captured during rush-hour traffic in downtown Miami. (Apparently few 1910 folks bothered to wonder how the world's largest python *got* to downtown Miami in the first place.)

Anyway, the young reporter found out that the monster python (which apparently was slowly starving to death in its cage) had actually been purchased by von Moser from a New York zoo.

They said that he had gotten quite a good buy on Mr. Python, because it had been refusing to eat its meals down at the zoo, and *was* slowly starving to death.

So much for the grand dreams of another member of the Deposed European Nobility Scam Club of Florida. It was said that at one time, there were more deposed European noble people in Palm Beach alone than there were on the entire European continent.

Old von Moser is way back in the ranks behind fishing guide/promoter Charlie Thompson. Charlie was the fellow who got the rights to the world's largest fish. It was a twenty-six-thousand-pound whale shark, taken on a derrick chain during the building of Flagler's Overseas Railroad. Charlie put that sucker on a railroad flatcar and hauled it all over the country, collecting those dimes from folks. (It may have been a quarter by that time, considering inflation and all.)

So let's set up a Scam Land Hall of Fame, with German nobleman von Moser and old Mr. Python, Charlie Thompson and the world's biggest fish, Prince Michael of Austria, and Willie Popham. And don't forget about our ostrich egg ranch fellows, too. And down the next aisle, we'll have Danny and the inmates, the $50 tipper in the Rolls, "Dicky" Bolles, and Joe the piano man. Maybe we'll also have Mindy and Jeff fighting the promoter of the Let's Pretend Airline. There's lots more coming up, but the hustlers really deserve to be recognized.

Especially if you see them coming.

20

Grandaddy's Rail Rule: If the Rails Don't Come to Your Town, Mister, You Don't Have a Town

A WHILE BACK WE TOUCHED BRIEFLY on the railroads and the rail barons, and their role in the birthing of Florida. This section does not mean to imply in any way that the railroad builders were trying to perpetrate a scam on the fledgling state. It's rather a study of the effect of pure, awesome power, when such power is wielded in a negotiation of any kind . . . in this case, land for the railroad builders.

In modern times, we can only imagine the raw power held by the rail barons. Indeed, that power extended to their investment bankers, their backers, their political representatives in the legislature, and all the rest.

Heck, among the actual rail barons themselves, there were really only four major players. That's right, four! Of course that's plus old David Yulee, who sort of got the whole thing started. But you'll hear more about him a little later on. We're talking about four major players who could move their chess pieces around their very own personal fifty-eight-thousand-square-mile game board, just about any way they chose to.

With this much power, they could virtually call any shot they wished for any deal, and divide the state into whatever pieces they wanted.

That's why I decided that the rails deserved a bit more than just a cursory glance.

First, the four major players:

Henry Flagler was probably the most overwhelming single influence on the development of 1890s Florida. His companies, his workers, and his Standard Oil millions enabled him to put his rails and hotels down the Atlantic coast from Fernandina to Key West.

The "other Henry," Henry Plant, a somewhat self-made rail express agent, began cutting his way across the state to run his rails and hotels down the Gulf Coast, ending in Fort Myers.

S. Davies Warfield developed smaller rails which would eventually connect the two giants, including his rail lines from the Tampa Bay area through Okeechobee and Indiantown.

And William D. Chipley, who had started out as a manager for the Louisville and Nashville rail properties in the Florida Panhandle, grew to become "the other railroader." Chipley chose to run his rails westward from Appalachicola to Pensacola. (A very smart move, since he was virtually to have that region all to himself.)

And about David Yulee . . . remember I mentioned that Internal Improvements Board, the one that handed out the land goodies to the rail companies, and the two railroad company presidents who were *on* the board? Well, Yulee was one of those presidents. He probably helped the whole idea get started for his Florida Railroad Company.

Meanwhile, back at the old legislature in Tallahassee, one news writer summed up the times rather succinctly. He wrote, "Our society is topsy-turvy. Liquor flows freely everywhere. Crime is rampant. Our money seems to be going back to Washington, and we'd like to get some of it back." (Sounds just like last week, doesn't it?) Could be any generation, but the writer was putting those words to paper in the capital town of a brand-new state, just at the beginning of Florida's career.

It was 1845, Florida's birth year.

From the mid-1800s into the beginning of the 1900s, by simply studying the moves of Flagler, Plant, Chipley, and Warfield—and their agents—you could plot the growth of any particular corner of Florida you chose. You could virtually map the progress, the land development, and the influx of new people, and even lay out a timetable for that particular area's growth. (The people would be arriving by rail, of course, with many of them being sold land by the rail companies.)

At that time, Florida only had *one* tiny, twenty-one-mile-long railroad—and it was from 1834. It was an old mule train, running from tiny Tallahassee to an even tinier St. Marks down on the Gulf Coast.

So the stage was definitely set for a show, and the rail barons were just about to give one.

The little people were going to get to watch the beginnings of what some call Florida's first great "land grab." The rail barons were going to get to divvy up millions of acres of state-owned land.

And the little people were also going to get to learn some of those good old Grandaddy's Rules.

The land awards were originally conceived—we may assume—as strips of free land on which the rail kings (I've promoted them from just barons) were to plant their rails. However, human nature (the only kind we have) being what it is, the land grants began to grow . . . and grow . . . and grow. The awards gradually became considered (by both sides) as either a reward, a bonus, an incentive, a divine right, or all of the above.

Within a short time, as I told you before, the idea of land awards had grown so that those rail-builders might expect tracts of land up to *six miles wide* for each mile of track they would promise to build.

And now, Yulee, along with the other rail president on the board, Dr. Baldwin of the Florida Atlantic and Gulf Central, plus the governor and some other state officials, came up with an *additional* bonus plan. Check this out.

They voted to give the rail boys, in addition to their six-mile-wide right-of-way, a $10,000 bonus for each mile of track to be laid by the companies! Boy howdy!

And in 1879, the munificent good old boys increased the goodies again. This time, they expanded the *size* of the land grants "to exceed the previous six-mile limit." By this time, many grants were made to railroaders and their rail lobbies that were far removed from the actual rail right-of-way route—sometimes even far away from the area to be served by the railroad. It was a happy-go-lucky sort of millionaire maker machine, once you got into the loop and were a part of the club.

It was these land bonuses which some consider to be among the very first of Florida's earliest scams. Maybe some small-time siding boys or penny-stock boiler rooms existed somewhere in Florida, but we hadn't heard about them yet.

Scam or no, decades later, major court cases were to grow out of all this fun and games. Various state factions began to demand tax satisfaction from some of the earlier rail companies for largesse they had received at the hands of that Internal Improvements Board of long ago. As eminent historian Charlton Tebeau once related, Henry Flagler was said to have received, as "right-of-way" for his West Palm Beach-Miami single rail line, about a half-million acres of Florida's 1896 Gold Coast. And he was so shrewd, he gave free train rides to anyone who bought some of that land from him—land that he had gotten from the state for free, mind you. I guess he figured he could afford it.

Large landowners with land near the proposed rails were often happy to give land for rights-of-way in order to bring the rails to their town.

Let me point out that the rails, of course, were the lifeline of the infant Florida. Rails were to bring thousands upon thousands of settlers, supplies, workers, jobs, and crops.

And in Florida, the railroad was bringing all these

wonders into areas where none had existed before, and where the region might have been almost totally inaccessible prior to its arrival. (We had a thing they called swamp.)

This point alone provided the basis for virtually any action taken by any board, commission, or candidate, any moves they had to make to secure the position of the railroads.

They had probably heard of Grandaddy's Rail Rule: If the rails don't come to your town, mister, you don't have a town.

21

The Consumer Advocate Con

NOW LET'S SEE. WE'VE TOUCHED on land sales, stock sales, pyramid schemes, boiler rooms, "telemarketing," oil wells, siding games, air-conditioning inspections, and I don't know what.

We've visited Popham's three thousand Oyster Huts, the ostrich egg ranch empire, and "Maggot Mile."

I reckon we've covered almost every kind of scam and con you could ever dream up.

Now what if there was a service specifically designed to help folks in their time of trouble, when they've just been scammed, conned, swindled, or bamboozled? You know, sort of like a counseling service that would offer to help you get your money back, or maybe get some satisfaction from the smooth-talking air-conditioning guys, or the roofing or siding people, or the good-looking investment counselor who sold you those penny stocks . . . or *anybody* who had sold you a bill of goods. It would be like the advertising guy who went into psychiatry and ran ads saying satisfaction guaranteed or your mania back.

Wouldn't that be a good idea? Let's assume that such a service *did* exist. Now what if that service began to go sour, and the operators began taking advantage of folks in their discombobulated state of mind? It would be easy enough to do, what with folks all upset and all.

Oh come on now. This is silly. That really could never happen, could it? How could anything as dumb as that ever fool people, especially after they'd just been burned? Everybody knows that lightning never strikes twice in the same place . . . and once bitten, twice shy . . . and that there's really nothing new under the sun . . . and all those other great truisms.

Right? Sorry, bunky, but *wrong!*

In fact, the incredible truths about con victims simply outdistance all judgment and logic. And Albert Crenshaw of *The Washington Post* has the facts to prove it.

Crenshaw, in an article, did a remarkable job of exploring the mindset of the scam victim. He uncovered a unique *new* scam. (Here we thought there was nothing new under the sun.)

You may find this hard to believe, but it's hard, cold fact. And according to the Florida Department of Law Enforcement, it's happening regularly to Florida's host of seniors, just as it's happening in massive doses in other regions across America that possess similar demographics.

The scam is perpetrated by scam artists or businessmen operating at the edge of the law. They pretend to be "consumer advocate" folks, offering to try to help scam victims—sometimes even their *own* victims—recover what they have lost in a recent scam experience.

Hard to believe? Certainly. But scammers actually do pose as consumer helpers, representatives of various state agencies, even paralegals or law enforcement and consumer protection people. They call up the victim and offer to help. And the truly unbelievable part is that the victim, who may not even have reported being swindled, doesn't appear to wonder how the caller got his or her name!

And even more astonishing is that they don't wonder how the caller could have learned so many details of their experience.

These appear to be the parts of our human nature (but,

again, it's the only kind we have) which continue to mystify the experts.

Crenshaw's digging uncovered the facts that lightning often *does* strike twice—even three or four times; people, once victimized, are apparently even *more,* rather than less, likely to be hoodwinked and bamboozled again by a smooth-talking con artist—sometimes, incredibly enough, by the *same* con artist; and the smooth-talking con persons apparently will exchange or even sell "victim lists" among themselves. The more expert cons have gone back two, three, and more times to the same trough, scoring on the same victims over and over again.

The con artists have learned that, after having been hoodwinked, the victim seems to be willing to reach out to anyone who appears sympathetic and who seems willing to help recoup the victim's losses, even a small part of them.

While the victim will not be thinking along these lines, the scam artist certainly will. The scam artist knows all about the victim's loss, since he, or she, maybe along with some accomplices, probably played a role in bringing that loss about.

For a "recovery fee" (sometimes a percentage of the recovery, paid in advance, of course), the con promises to recoup the victim's entire loss. This operation is sometimes referred to as a "recovery company."

Attorney Robert Rex of Boca Raton tells me that there are firms and promoters who solicit scam victims as clients, much like a realtor might seek a listing. Having secured a list of perhaps a dozen or more such "clients," the promoter will then solicit a firm of lawyers and ask them to take on all the cases. The promoter may have made promises to the victims which may or may not be possible to fulfill.

There are others who are just plain old bandits, but without the mask and gun. These scammers apparently get their information from the original con artists and then call the victims, suggesting that they can recover some of the victim's losses for a fee. The sad part about this operation is that these rascals will simply file a consumer complaint on behalf of the victim with the appropriate state authorities, and then let the matter drop. Of course, the con is that the victim could have filed the same complaint with state authorities at no cost at all.

In yet *another* twist, the original crook sometimes moves away or leaves town. You may have heard this referred to in the vernacular as "skipping town." (See Grandaddy's small Rule #13-a which reminded us, don't never go into bin-ness with a feller named Skip.)

The con will then actually *sell* a list of his previous victims to a new scammer who is coming in to work the territory. (We may assume with lots of helpful marginal notes about the victims included in that list.)

The world of scam goes on and on.

22

Cons, Cons, and More Cons

SOME GRAND AND WISE OLD POET once said, "Breathes there a man with soul so dead, who never to himself hath said . . . If I only had a million dollars!" And you could add, Then I could have (fill in the dream of your choice: exotic cars, drugs, ladies, fancy homes, yachts, motorcycles, *eye*-talian suits and custom-made shoes, 747s . . . any or all of the above.)

No matter what the dream, somebody, somewhere has dreamed it.

The con man or lady depends on that secret innermost wish to help make their con work successfully. The con artist *knows* he can count on the fantasy of what each of us would do with our treasure.

My friends at the Associated Press uncovered a guy who had a plumbing business up in Philadelphia someplace. This guy had actually rigged some kind of "call-forwarding" device on his phone that would divert incoming phone calls from other local plumbing contractors' telephones directly to his own. He was literally stealing customers right out from under the noses of his competitors. (Don't you suppose some of those folks are *still* trying to figure out how this dude worked all this out?)

This scam eventually found its way to Florida, where it

was uncovered just as it was getting underway. Meanwhile, the Philadelphia guy's scam was working wonderfully . . . perhaps too well. It finally crashed when a customer of one of the victimized companies called that company to compliment the owner on the good job his workers had done in her home over the previous holiday weekend.

The boss informed the caller that his men hadn't worked that weekend, and the scam began to unravel. The culprit was eventually charged with theft by deception. (Not too sure what other kind of theft there is, but no matter.) He was also charged with criminal attempt, unlawful use of a computer, criminal trespass, and—how about this one—impersonating an employee! (Man, I didn't know they could get you for that. That'd almost be like catching somebody working while on company time. Disgraceful!)

Now it's only a few short steps to the ancient but still workable bank-examiner scam.

This is the one where a nice-talking fellow in a spiffy suit comes up to you in the bank and asks you to withdraw some money from your account "to help the examiners catch a thieving bank employee." This oldie-but-goodie has been around so long that by this time, those little warning bells should be playing "Auld Lang Syne" in your ear. However, it shows no sign of being tossed aside by the new generations of the con fraternity.

It's hard to believe the lengths that a con will go to, seeking that elusive something for nothing that my grandaddies told us about.

How about the guys who actually hand-sifted through giant trash dumpsters just to find an occasional, discarded credit card?

Speaking of elaborate plans, we must turn again to ace reporter Fred Schulte. Fred describes a category called "fly and buy." He spotlights some scammers in Fort Lauderdale who were selling—ready?—*telephone booths.*

Now this was not just any old telephone booth, but your

very own telephone booth. I suppose you could have your name engraved right on it if you wanted.

But listen to this. These guys said that you could buy hundreds of them if you wanted to. The scammers—according to their four-color brochures—would pick out your locations, install your phone booths for you, maintain and repair them, even collect the quarters from the coin-slots for you . . . all for a small fee.

It was truly an incredible opportunity!

But wait, there's more! And here comes the mind-boggling part that starts a tiny drop of cider sloshing around in your ear. Folks would see a little newspaper ad in Pitchfork, Wyoming, or Bugtussle, Arkansas, and be instantly galvanized into action.

They would feverishly call an enticing 800 number to inquire about this phone booth deal. It sounded almost too good to be true. (Chime! Tinkle!) And *then* they found out that the Lauderdale folks would actually *fly* you to Florida to see the plant for yourself, *totally free!* Hey, you couldn't go wrong with a deal like that, now could you?

They would actually meet you at the airport, I suppose limo you to the company, and take you on a tour through the plant. Here you would see sales reps calling all over the country, selling phone booths to people. Man, you were actually watching a boiler room in operation and didn't know it.

Then you would tour the plant and see rows of nice-looking people wearing handsome white smocks, working on what looked like telephone innards with computers all winking and blinking like crazy along the assembly line. Then you'd see long rows of great big cartons of phone booths, waiting to be shipped out . . . and man, you were ready to sign up!

Now these fellows were not into penny-ante stuff. Folks would hand over their checks—maybe $10,000, $15,000, $24,000—as much as they had. They would then smile broadly and head back to Pitchfork (or Bugtussle), knowing that they had finally found the pot of gold at the end of the rainbow, and had put one over on those slick dudes down in Fort Lauderdale.

And they had even gotten a free trip to Florida on a big, shiny airplane.

Trouble was, once they got back home to Pitchfork, they wouldn't ever hear from Fort Lauderdale—or their $24,000—again. They'd call and call. Nobody would ever return their phone calls. They received no phone booths in the mail, or on a truck, or nohow.

And the folks would say, But I *saw* the assembly lines and the phone booths being packed to be shipped out. I *know* it was a good deal.

So here comes the cider part. As Schulte describes, the scammers turned out to have bought about a dozen old telephone booths for a couple hundred bucks for the "workers" to work on. They were strictly window dressing and the smock-wearers were just wiggling wires back and forth. And the computers they saw were mockups, wired to keep winking and blinking like crazy to simulate some exciting stuff going on.

But the grand finale to the scam, those huge cartons holding finished phone booths ready for shipment, were actually filled with concrete blocks they got from a construction site. Man! How about *that* for attention to detail and master planning!

As Fred tells it, the scammers had the whole scam down to a fine science. They had code names for each step of the way in this major-league, post-graduate, Ph.D.-level con.

At the beginning came the "first pitch." This was followed by the "puffers," the sales pros who puffed up the investment plan. Then came the "singers," who sang the praises of the other investors' smarts. If the mark dragged his feet, then came the "owner's close," where the mark thought he was meeting one of the owners of the company.

When they got backlash—threats from bamboozled investors—these were called "heat calls."

It was truly a master scam by top professionals. Any time somebody will fly you to Florida to inspect their plant and check out their product, you *know* it's got to be a good deal. Just make sure you have your list of Grandaddy's Rules in your satchel—especially that Rule #6.

As a matter of fact, one of Papa Knight's small rules (I never even bothered to number these) would apply well in this "fly-and-buy" scam. The rule was: You never really know just how much you can do . . . until you try to *undo* some of what you've done.

23

How to Outsmart the Boiler-Room Boys; or, Do Unto Others Before They Do Unto You

WE LIVE IN THE AGE of Big Brother, of government bureaus, commissions, and bureaucrats watching over us all. With this there comes the predictable attitude among many individuals that Big Brother will take care of us all, that the government will watch out for us from cradle to grave.

That's one of the reasons it's so refreshing to run across a Vern Thornton.

Vern is an interesting guy. He used to be a chief deputy sheriff in Broward County. (Remember how Fort Lauderdale was a contender for capital of scam honors?) Well, that's where Vern was, so he knew firsthand what was going down.

Then he worked with the State Department of Corrections for a while. And as he began to approach the "sunny side of seventy," he began to realize how many of Florida's seniors were spending some of their sunset years at risk, suffering at the hands of Florida's ever-expanding ranks of scammers.

For example, some three thousand seniors were bilked out of more than *five million dollars* in "grand prize scams." They were told that they had just won a big prize of some kind and must send a small amount of money to cover taxes, shipping, and handling.

In another variation, they're told that they have won the lottery, and a courier will stop by to pick up a "good-faith deposit."

So Vern, being a guy who likes to take action, decided to do something.

Vern, along with some buddies, began to take an active role in the "Seniors vs. Crime" project, which had been founded by the state attorney general's office along with the American Association of Retired Persons.

Their group, which they had nicknamed the "Sleuthing Seniors," grew to some 350 strong in Palm Beach County and around Lake Worth. On their own, they began to take on assignments helping ferret out scams and swindles which might be perpetrated on their members by area businesses.

The organization often receives funding assistance from companies in the area which have had to settle claims against—or on behalf of—victims in one way or another.

Funds for the Sleuthing Seniors have also come from the various state fines imposed on the scammers. In one case, fines were paid by a major insurance company for allegedly selling life insurance as a retirement plan.

In another instance, money came from a Sears, Roebuck & Co. settlement of charges that it had misled auto-repair customers.

As Vern Thornton, head sleuth, said, "Sometimes the companies that defraud us are the ones that pay for our activities and our program."

Beth Reinhard, staff member of the *Palm Beach Post,* wrote, "The senior sleuths do an amazing amount of detective drone work. They sift through junk mail looking for bogus charities and companies. Sometimes, they put in many office hours logging suspicious phone calls and contest offers."

The most prevalent scams on seniors use the omnipresent telemarketing approach. This is so because retired people often have free time to chat on the phone and are sometimes willing to talk with total strangers who call.

In fact, the FBI estimates that "telemarketers" spend up to a third of their time zeroing in on senior citizens. The "master closers" and specialists can generate up to hundreds of cold calls per day simply by going through their purchased lists of seniors in a given locale.

Counselors to seniors' groups advise a remarkably simple plan that is *guaranteed* to reduce the risk of being ripped off in a phone scam.

One of the approaches recommended is the advance preparation of a polite but firm rejection to use when called by a solicitor. If necessary, people should memorize the statement.

There are several variations, but, "I'm sorry, we do not consider phone solicitations," followed by hanging up the phone, will be the most effective. If you wish, you may add thank you, but the hang-up is the most important part.

Now remember, on this plan you *must* ignore your natural curiosity about the caller's subject matter, product, or benefit—even if it's "your prize." ("Your prize" should be added to your Key Words List.)

Simply remember, the caller is sitting in a boiler room somewhere that's filled with other callers, each touching an automatic dialing mechanism that instantly, upon your hang-up, dials the next number in a computer database. (Now you didn't *really* think those guys actually looked up *your* number and called you personally because they wanted to find out how you were, did you?)

Ahhh, the wonders of modern technology. And we haven't even gotten to cyberspace yet. This is practically the old Chisholm Trail at this point. Machines let the seller make maximum use of every second of time, delivering that opening line greeting hundreds of times within a single *hour.*

The crucial point for the callee to remember is that your hang-up is really not going to hurt someone's feelings. By the time you've gotten back to your dinner table, the dialing machine can already have dialed two or three more numbers.

I've heard of master callers, working major-league national phone rooms with automatic speed-dialers, who are able to generate up to a *thousand* tries in a single—long—day.

Now, out of that astonishing number, the master closer will capture the imagination of an amazing number of prospects, probably through the possession of an overpowering empathy that works well over a phone line. Any good salesperson can verify that good *listening* is half of successful selling.

Anyway, within a single hour, the master closer will captivate twenty to thirty people, and may actually generate some kind of positive action from ten or more of these prospects. An "action" might be simply getting the prospect to agree to a personal visit by a "closer." The caller generally makes a commission for each appointment produced, and sometimes a bonus for each appointment which results in a "close," or order.

So simple arithmetic figures up about one hundred live prospects produced by a single master telemarketer in a single day of calling.

With a top-flight, greedy, motivated telemarketer who really wants life's good things and can hang in there for ten to eleven hours at a stretch, we're up to about a thousand calls per day.

By the way, that "telemarketer" buzzword grew out of the 1960s buzzword "marketing," which grew out of the 1950s and '40s college courses that didn't want to call it "selling" because none of the kids would enroll. And all this grew out of the post-depression era of the 1930s when those kids' daddies learned that "salesman" (meaning door-to-door salesman) was considered by many to be a dirty word in our culture.

In case you've wondered, this is how many post-World War II marketing majors in college *backed* into sales jobs as they found out that that was what the buzzword had really meant all along.

Anyway, keep that thousand-a-day/one-hundred-an-hour set of numbers in your mind for future reference. I'll come back to them later.

Like every business, the telemarketing/boiler-room industry will have its superstars and its "also-rans": the folks who try hard but just don't quite have that burning drive that propels them into the big leagues. One young stud in the biz told me that he could easily earn a quarter of a million dollars annually, just by sitting at the phone ten hours a day. He called it his "Burning Motivational Work" ethic. He said he kept those three initials on a pad in front of him at all times to remind him of the things he really liked in his life.

This is nothing new; it's no big scoop. Throughout the entire sales profession in America, scam or straight, it has long been an accepted axiom that about 80 percent of all sales is produced by the top 20 percent of America's salespersons.

Now, if you've ever wondered at the reluctance of a caller to follow your suggestion and just put it in the mail, there is a sort of unwritten law about this in the boiler-room industry.

It probably began to develop with the growth of those massive nationwide penny-stock sales campaigns in the 1960s and 1970s, when phone canvassing was new.

This was where some tiny, totally unknown stock would start out at maybe ten cents per share in the morning, and by nightfall, hundreds of callers generating thousands of calls would have churned the stock up to a *dollar!* (Remember, for those early morning ten-cent buyers, this would be a thousand percent gain by sundown.) And all from master telemarketers making those thousands of calls.

The rule said simply, If you mail, you fail.

And I suppose every mom and pop out there who got up from their meatloaf and mashed potatoes about 6:30 each evening to go over to answer the telephone can understand that.

Grandaddy's Rule #9-b (a small rule) will help span the chasm from that little one-hundred-call-per-hour level to the cyberspace age. The gods must have been looking over Papa Johnson's shoulder when he developed his secret for successful selling.

He said the rule in selling is quite simple: Either do it better, or faster, or *longer* than the next feller, and you'll always make out all right.

Cyberspace . . . here we come.

24

An Introduction to Cyberspace; or, When Computers Take Over TV, It'll Be Time to Dredge the Channel

THERE ARE PROBABLY ONLY A couple major times in America's history that millions and millions of Americans joined together and sort of conspired to break the law of the land. Whether the law was just or not is not a point for us to consider. It's simply that a majority of Americans apparently felt that a particular law was not worthwhile . . . even though they, themselves, had voted to pass the law.

The first case is easy: Prohibition, of course, with bootleg hooch, the speakeasy joints, bathtub gin, and rum-runners all helping develop the gangster era in America. Florida grew to become a major port of entry for bootleggers during Prohibition.

The other, far less noticeable, and far less damaging, movement occurred in the citizens-band (CB) radio era. In the 1960s and 1970s, millions of Americans—without even realizing they were doing so—became amateur radio announcers and DJs. They were broadcasting on their very own private (often unlicensed) citizens-band radios in their cars.

Virtually everyone adopted a fake name, or "handle," to assure anonymity. This way the game was always completely safe, since no listener ever knew the identity of a caller (at least until sophisticated call girls began using CBs to solicit "johns" along the open road, urging them to meet at convenient truck-stops up ahead).

Often, the Federal Communications Commission in Washington found it could not really trace who had licenses to broadcast and who didn't.

At one point, the communications press in D.C. said that it was next to impossible to try to enforce the licensing of CB radios, since they estimated that there were probably about twelve million of them already in use without licenses. The FCC just sort of gave up on the project.

The fad soon ran its course and faded into America's novelty history along with the hula hoop and the Beatles wig—except for diehard, good-buddy truckers and semi-trailer knights of the road.

Actually, none of the above constitutes a scam of any major measure. The real meat of the issue is the millions of drivers on the highways who used CBs to break America's speed laws.

This conspiracy indeed was to become a scam of enormous proportions. The game included CB reports to other drivers about speed traps, "smokies," "eye-in-the-sky" helicopters, "bears," "bears in the air," "convoys," and the like. It grew to become a gigantic game all across the land, sort of like Prohibition but without the machine-gun massacres.

There was simply no end to the creative ideas leaping from the fertile minds of CBers on how to break the speed laws.

It involved millions of otherwise law-abiding citizens.

As such, it was to become the second-grandest law-breaking game in America's history, following Prohibition.

Now, why bring up these two grand games at all?

Well, we're about to see that both of these, plus probably every scam ever dreamed up by America's con fraternity, will quickly fade into the mists of memory in our America of Tomorrow.

All of the law-breakers, all of the Prohibition bootleggers, all of the cons ever since . . . all rolled up together into a giant ball . . . won't amount to hardly anything within the next couple of decades in the con man's dream world, the computer age of scam.

It's like comparing the thousand-call-per-day machine to the old-fashioned sidewalk hustler in the checkered suit with the three walnut shells and the pea.

So welcome to cyberspace, that fascinating, bewildering, awe-inspiring, mind-bending, even sometimes amusing, tomorrowland moniker.

It's the handle invented by writers, editors, and commentators—and computer geeks—all across the land.

The word itself, according to resident computer/cyberspace genius Glen Rovinelli, comes to us down a long, convoluted road from "cybernetics": the science of electronically amplifying and magnifying the human senses. If that gets too involved for you, just remember TV's "Six Million Dollar Man." He was the dude with all his muscles pumped up by all that scientific equipment plugged into his bones after his accident in space. Remember? Well that's sort of the way it works. At least that's what Glen says.

Or how about the "heads-up" displays in today's supersonic fighter planes, where the pilot simply "sees" all his gauges *inside* his helmet without actually looking down at his instrument panel . . . and where the complete instrument panel simply follows his gaze wherever he turns his glance?

Or how about special eyeglasses where the wearer can operate a computerized printer just by blinking an eye?

Anyway, you begin to catch my drift.

Now it does get complicated. My grandaddies would have had a hard time putting some of their rules to it. But some of them will still apply, even in our speed-of-light scam world of tomorrow out here in cyberspace.

Here, Glen tells me, we find an electronic community—a sort of town square—where folks may meet, chat, ponder, debate, query, buy, and sell, just about any time they choose, and from all corners of the planet. You can even put a nickel in the jukebox and play your favorite tunes, some old favorites and some of the new ones as well—all on your computer screen. It'll be music on TV, but without the TV. As a matter of fact, the friendly old TV screen could become the stereopticon slide of the twenty-first century if we don't watch out. (And it's okay if you don't remember the stereopticon slide. It was a long time ago.)

Anyway, human nature being what it is, folks have immediately begun to figure out ways to con, scam, swindle, and bamboozle each other via this new electronic wonder, the computer screen. Man, that sucker can do things you've never seen done before . . . and all in "real time." (Now that's another great computer-age buzzword. Loosely translated, it means "right now" in OldSpeak.)

For you Underwood manual typewriter folks, that means that in the same instant (or almost the same instant) that you type something on your screen, your pen-pal/buddy in Wherever, Utah, is going to *see it!*

And that goes for your prospect in Copenhagen, Bombay, Rangoon, Innsbruck—or Wherever, Utah—as well. He—or she—is going to see that message right away.

Now when we expand the scam artists' playing field to encompass the entire planet, with any point reachable in seconds . . . and all in that spiffy real time I told you about . . . well *hot-cha!*

25

Cyberspace's Scam Potential; or, The Ten-Cent Chain Letter Times One Hundred Million

To try to get a clear picture of the wild and wacky world of cyberspace, at least as far as our scams are concerned, we need some sort of a plan of action.

First, let's take just a few ingredients of some of the good old scams and cons we've been talking about and some others we can think of, and mix them together.

Let's start first with the simple old-fashioned chain-letter scam. If you go back far enough, you'll remember a letter you or your folks got in the mail that promised that if you mailed copies of the letter to five of your dearest friends and placed a *dime* in each letter, you would eventually get back *five dollars* in the mail! Maybe going back that far is taxing your memory-banks a bit, but it used to happen just about that way.

Let's add some samples of various pyramid schemes, stock-selling cons, work-at-home hustles ("Stuff envelopes; earn thousands at home in your spare time!") . . . plus new and old get-rich-quick offers of virtually every kind the mind of man can conceive.

I think that we will find that in tomorrow's cyberspace, most state-of-the-art, high-tech scams will likely just be modern-day updates of the old familiar types above.

As reporters at the Associated Press have pointed out in

many articles, the con artists have just adopted the facilities of today's electronic communications as a means to seek out new prospects.

Whether it's the Internet, cyberspace, e-mail, on-line computer services, faxes, or worldwide bulletin boards, it's still just a very old message communicated in a new language.

Now, about those chain letters . . . listen to this: one bunch of modern-day scammers worked up an Internet chain-letter game. Their message on the old info-road, appearing on your personal computer (PC) screen (as well as on the screens of hundreds of thousands of others), called for you to do some specific things. First, you were to send them $5, which would sort of get the ball rolling. (Whatever happened to the dime?) (Now, if you're checking your Key Words List carefully, you'll find that this comes under the heading of "sending"; I warned you about that.)

Anyway, then they would send you a computer disk with the names and addresses of four other people to whom you were *also* supposed to send $5—each. The plot (and the cider) begins to thicken. (And by this time, almost any of Grandaddy's Rules should have begun to kick in.)

Once you had done all this, and only then, you were to add your own name to the disk. Well, *finally!* Now we're getting someplace.

The only trouble was, now you were supposed to go out and try to *sell* that disk to some new players.

This game promised that you could win up to $20,000 in twenty weeks if you played it right. (That is, if you did everything you were supposed to and followed every instruction to the letter.)

Boy howdy, just think what old Popham the Oyster King could have done with his porpoise-hide shoelaces and his delicious and nutritious Oyster Nip drinks if he'd only had a laptop and the Internet to play with.

We've come a long way, baby.

Probably the most popular thing among the simple folk will be the PC bulletin board. Here you'll find a group of folks with a common interest or concern. But remember, this is global. A "group" can be hundreds of thousands of people scattered around the planet. And where you have hundreds of thousands of people, scams are very likely to follow. You can almost sense it coming around the bend.

These so-called bulletin boards are just that—electronic, on-line bulletin boards with little messages soaring off into cyberspace to produce the pitch heard 'round the world.

One writer called it "tightly-focused information," much like your old corkboard bulletin board down at the foundry where guys would pin up little notes saying, Remington .410 for sale cheep.

As Rovenelli and our computer-store wizards tell us, with listservs, the server company will let you send and receive messages electronically; this is known as e-mail. Remember, that message may be sent to hundreds of thousands of folks simultaneously.

You're now on the worldwide party-line, friend . . . and the subject matter can be just about anything the mind of man can conjure up . . . from Caribbean shellfish and mollusks, to Art Hodes clarinet solos, to UFOs, to some tiny, little-known, brand-new stock issue you've never heard of that just came out that morning at ten cents per share. (Watch out now, here it comes.)

That's right . . . ten cents a share. And a nice-sounding gentleman, whose code name (back in CB days, we called it your handle) might be "Dude," posts a little note that says, our company is exploring a spiffy new miracle-fabric in our plant here in Chicopee that's going to replace the wheel. And we're all really excited about it.

Then his buddy, another nice-sounding geek, in Stuttgart, whose nickname might be "Stud," posts a little note saying, yeah, my brother-in-law knows all about that stuff. Your stock's hotter than a two-dollar pistol on

Saturday night over here. It just came out this morning at ten cents (or *kroner,* or *zlotys,* or whatever). (Now we're not too sure that folks from Stuttgart talk that way, but you get the idea.) Then a guy from Swaziland pipes in with, wow, ten *lilangeni,* eh? Can you get me some? And then another nice-sounding guy in, say, Seattle, says, hey, Dude, can you get me some too? And Dude in Chicopee says sure, my brother knows the president of the company . . . and then Dallas chimes in and says hey, what was the name of that stock, again? I know our guys in Tijuana will want to get in on some of this.

Meanwhile, you and thousands of other folks are watching all this take place on your own computer screen. And by dern if you don't decide to call your broker in the morning and order some of it too. And the first thing next morning, that little old ten-cent stock is burbling along around $3 a share. But you buy a whole bunch of it anyway, because you know it jumped up from ten cents in just twenty-four hours! Wow! What a break! You sure got in on the ground floor on this one, all right!

And the *next* morning it's trading at . . . ten cents a share. Because the company never existed in the first place, except mainly on paper and in the creative brains of the guys in Chicopee, Stuttgart, and Swaziland. (The guys in Seattle, Dallas, and Tijuana got taken, too—along with thousands of others.)

It might take five or six guys at various outposts around the planet to light your fire, but they'll get to you eventually. They'll be the scammers and you'll be the scammee, along with Dallas, Seattle, and Tijuana. And Grandaddy's Rules # 5 and #6 will, by now, have begun to tickle your ear.

And all it took was a little bunch of good old boys chatting up some little old stock they knew about, and the rest of the world was just eavesdropping.

As you can quickly discern, these good old boys aren't settling anymore for just a couple hundred form letters, or even several thousand phone calls over several months' time. They're going to touch hundreds of thousands of lives within a single instant.

As for cyberlaws, well, it's simply a whole new world of wonders, with a whole new world of questions—and few answers. In one instance, it was even debated as to whether an item on a PC bulletin board actually constituted a legal offer to sell or not. One commentator said it almost seemed like a gargantuan eavesdropping plan, sort of a twentieth-century economic and fiscal voyeurism.

Although the future may change a lot of the rules, at this writing, the on-line investment scams and the anticipated unlimited varieties of opportunity for Internet fraud will prove extremely difficult, if not impossible, to police effectively.

Try to grasp the sheer enormity of the communications evolution we are facing, just within the coming decade! Imagine the most elementary capabilities of the Internet. Now, try to project the rewards that are possible for even the most simple-minded scammer.

All we need to do is look at the numbers.

One Associated Press survey estimated that, at any given moment, there will probably be more than five thousand messages (cybersells) available to viewers on their PC screens—on just one subject alone.

Further, this is just on *one* of the major on-line services. Now figure that some *seven thousand services* are said to exist, just at this writing.

You can imagine all those seven thousand Internet companies pumping out bulletin board items like that little stock in Stuttgart to fifty million potential marks around the planet on their full-color PC screens. Now you have some concept of what the real numbers can be.

And that's just *now;* the whole shebang is just getting started.

My Atlanta computer adviser Bruce Brawner says that the

Library of Congress Internet site might currently log tens of thousands of calls in a single *day* for its bottomless computer files of information on a virtually endless array of topics.

And one last "remember": all of this is with only about thirty million PCs in use. The global world of scam will know no bounds, as some estimates show about a million or more new members hooking up every month.

By the way, since the Internet has such an incredible reach, that old hundred-calls-per-hour/thousand-calls-per-day telephone boiler room will probably become obsolete. I really hated to be the one to bring you this news, but somebody had to do it.

Believe it or not, there may come a day when you will complete your entire dinner without having a single boiler-room stranger on the phone saying, Hi Bill, how are ya this evening?

And then you'll sit down at your computer, and your e-mail box will be full.

Papa Knight would have loved the Internet.

26

Cyberspace Scams Part II

ONE OF THE SIMPLEST AND most successful of all scams is presently running the world over, from Florida to the frozen tundra of Siberia.

According to reports from the Associated Press, it incorporates the new high-tech PC bulletin board techniques I just mentioned.

However, when we strip away the cyber-veneer, it still turns out to be the tried-and-true pyramid scheme.

There are reports of duped investors in Moscow, of all places, losing their life savings.

The pyramid scheme is one of the very oldest—and most successful—scams in the world of financial fraud. Now remember, in a pyramid scheme, promoters rely on an ever-widening network of new investors, whose money is then used to pay "returns" to previous investors. All of this creates a happy illusion of success where no success may actually exist.

Pyramids are now coming alive in a brand-new showplace—your computer screen, via the global game board, the Internet!

Here we might find major players in, say, Tibet, or Oslo, or Two-Egg, Florida.

One of the latest schemes, in the 1990s, involved a

computer chain letter using e-mail, which promised a payoff of some $60,000 for a $5 investment.

This game was similar to the one we previously looked at, only in this case it was perhaps aimed at the less affluent. In this one, each prospect, staring at untold riches hidden in that magic electronic box of wonders, was told to send $1 to each of five people on the e-mail list. The mark was then told to add his or her own name to the bottom of the list and send that off.

These promoters were apparently hustling their shell-game by posting a simple notice on their worldwide folding table under some kind of a label, such as Make Lots of Money Real Fast Without Doing Anything, or maybe even a catchy one-word title such as Money. My researchers tell me that this title will often capture a lot of attention quickly—almost like leaving a $50 tip down at the old barbershop every Friday.

The promoters used randomly-chosen PC bulletin boards, which exposed their gospel to hundreds of thousands of likely marks along the old information superhighway.

One of the most telling parts of this story is that many of these folks, when queried later, indicated that they didn't recognize the program as a chain letter at all, let alone a scam of any kind. Folks said, How could it have been a scam? I saw it right there on my computer screen.

This proves, perhaps, two major theories: that some folks have discovered a new deity to worship and that Barnum, after all, is still right.

And since the desire to fulfill the dream of finding that elusive pot of gold at the end of the rainbow recognizes no international boundaries, we turn to Russia. Officials have uncovered a Russian investment company which they have categorized as the typical American pyramid scheme. They indicate that thousands of investors in that country are being victimized by their comrades.

It's probably just like that old saw about the investor, seeing a rising stock, screaming at his broker, "Buy! Buy! Buy!" Then, as the stock collapsed, he screamed, "Sell! Sell! Sell!" And the broker replied, "To whom?"

Another of the international schemes was a European company called Kings Club. The firm, again using the wonders of the PC venue, quickly raised more than a million dollars from investors in eighteen states across America. Florida was well-represented on this roster.

There's only about one category remaining that can possibly parallel—or even exceed—the titillation of investing in cyberspace. What do you think that little item could be?

Your rapid eye movement gave you away—you guessed it. S-E-X!

Sure enough, the computer scams have quickly found their way into the boudoir. As one voyeur/mark put it, "Man, you can find anything you like on that little screen . . . I mean *anything!*"

Anyway, the wonderful differences of our two genders quickly grew to surpass just about anything the glittering world of cyberspace had had to offer up to that point, rivaling even *money!* It was simply the newest and the best: sex, right on your computer screen.

The scammers quickly realized that they had tapped into another motherlode of riches, there for the taking.

Now, regular phone sex was already pretty popular. In one case, a fellow in Washington, D.C., somewhere, found his phone bills laden with numerous calls to a mysterious coded phone number in Ohio. That number turned out to be a relay system of some sort to another number somewhere in Russia. Each of the calls charged to his phone bill had been an audio sexual adventure full of suggestive conversation—for his kids.

It seems his teen-agers had been hustled into making the calls by friends who had been hustled by promoters . . . and so forth and so on.

But sex on the computer is even more popular. You can find almost every smut magazine on the Internet these days, giving you (and your kids) instant access to full-color soft-core, hard-core, and pure rotgut porn, any hour of the day or night—and in the privacy of your very own home.

Parents' reactions have helped create another new technology in response to all this which will eventually be able to screen and block out porn sites, but that's still a little ways off.

So now the Better Business Bureaus all over the land again come into play.

Ronald Stephens, president of the West Palm Beach bureau, tells me of plans for all of the 181 bureau offices across America to eventually be able to link up with each other via computer to share instant data on new or recurring scams.

Some commentators have suggested that we should put up a Proceed with Caution sign as we approach the worldwide info-highway, since we really don't know where it will all lead us or what incredible scams may lurk just around the bend.

Other people say, in essence, So what else is new? Boosters say, why ban sex from just the Internet? It will still be on radio, TV, and records; in movies, our homes, comic books, magazines, and postcards; and anywhere else we care to look.

The scam, says the opposition, is that cyberspace will simply be pandering to the lowest possible common denominator of our culture.

The pandering will be done by hustlers who are shoving their particular brand of con onto your computer screen. The good news is that *you* still hold the "clicker."

If either grandaddy had had a rule for it, he would have probably said . . . it still takes two to tango.

27

The Media Zoo; or, Due to Circumstances Beyond Our Control, the Light at the End of the Tunnel Has Been Temporarily Turned Off

ALTHOUGH WE'VE BRIEFLY TOURED THE wondrous world of cyberspace, including a little computer fraud and some of its ramifications, we haven't even touched on the media world of today and the role it will play in our computer scams of tomorrow.

Once we plunge into Future World, with the Internet and high-tech communications systems, where even our old TV may become obsolete, it's almost hard to come back down to earth. Gosh! Remember old radio and TV?

When it comes to getting a *license* for a radio or TV station, the scammers have found a way to help.

In one case, a company in Boca Raton was said to have collected about $16 million from some sixteen hundred investors nationwide for providing assistance in securing specialized mobile radio licenses.

The pitches were made over a period of about a year, via thirty-minute-long TV commercials, or "infomercials." (Now here is another developing media art-form that is just coming out of the starting blocks, but is coming up strong in the outside lane. Watch this new form run, once she hits her stride.)

By the time you read these words, we may have an entire network (or several) presenting nothing *but* continuous, half-hour- or hour-long infomercials for products for skin, hair, eyes, self-improvement, losing fat, gaining weight, making yourself over into Cary Grant, making big money at home, or buying fifty old houses with no money whatsoever of your own. No matter what the actual words may be, you get the idea.

But back to the media-license company. Investors paid one company about $7,000 each for help in attaining specialized, mobile radio transmitting licenses from the Federal Communications Commission in Washington, D.C. In fact, it would probably only have cost the applicants about $700 each to submit the application unassisted.

And even after forking over $7,000, the potential licensees were apparently not informed that they would need more than a third of a million dollars to build a broadcasting facility once the license was issued. Nor were they told that their facility had to be up and running within a specific time period, or the license would revert back to the FCC.

Officials indicated that little chance existed for these investors to ever recoup the bulk of their investments, nor was it likely that they would ever compete successfully in the mysterious media fraternity.

These folks had simply bought a long-term supply of Uncle Billy's Whiz-Bang Miracle Cough Syrup. They had also learned at least a couple of Grandaddy's Rules . . . and probably had found small amounts of cider in their ears.

This media-licensing case was in no way a one-of-a-kind undertaking. Just as with all scams, the idea quickly caught on with other operators, who swiftly moved into the field.

Another dynamic media-licensing company, operating in the same region, allegedly used deceptive advertising pitches to lure prospective investors into their net. They painted fantastic pictures of fortunes to be made at little or no risk, and with a minimum of up-front cash.

This one, known as the Chase McNulty Group, was one

of several entities which were said to have drawn more than a hundred million dollars from happy-go-lucky investors looking for that elusive pot of gold . . . but this one had a very special twist.

Chase McNulty returned to yesteryear for a nostalgia theme for their advertising, promotional materials, and sales pitches.

The promoters used their yesteryear theme to illustrate how easy it was to miss a golden, once-in-a-lifetime opportunity to invest in a new and exciting field, such as wireless cable.

Their writers told the tale of how, in the late 1800s, Alexander Graham Bell had tried to get his good friend, Mark Twain, to invest some $5,000 in a new venture. For his five thousand, Twain was to receive a substantial piece of a novel invention that Bell was trying to develop. He planned to call the invention a "telephone," and he planned to build a new company to try to sell the thing. His company was to be called the Bell Telephone Company.

Mark Twain, for all his monumental gifts, was known by his friends to make less than successful investments with all his royalties. Legendary folk hero Twain, drawing on his good, solid, midwestern common sense, was said to have replied to his friend that the idea of risking so much money on some kind of new toy, a *telephone,* for heaven's sake, would be "the height of rash speculation." And he wanted no part of it.

No one ever said they didn't write memorable advertising copy.

28

Publisher's Advice: Kid, Your Song Is Great, but Right Now, We're Looking for Trash

It's the 1950s again. And as Yogi Berra used to say, "It's deja vu all over again."

Anyway, it's the '50s . . . and every seventh car made in America is a station wagon. We hadn't sold our car-making souls to our international neighbors, yet. But we were getting ready to . . . the first little Beetle was soon to appear in your neighborhood, and guys would gather around the curb in the fall afternoon and stare at the thing.

A brand-new phenomenon was starting to appear that would change our lives forever . . . *and* play a major role in the scam business for decades to come. It was a new replacement for the thing we used to call a "neighborhood," and it was called a "suburb." And the comics were saying that by the time you got to where you could afford to move to one, they would move that sucker ten miles farther out.

And another new phenomenon appeared, mid-decade. It was called "Elvis." And a new thing began to hit the radio airwaves. New York DJ Alan Freed gave it a name; he called it "rock and roll." It was to change all the rules of making music which had been in force for a long, long time.

And we were just beginning to learn about the scam biz. We thought it was a brand-new thing. There were stories about the new siding salesmen, roof-inspection scandals, furnace-repair scams . . . even giant quiz-show scandals on TV where they actually told the contestants the answers in advance "to make it a better show." It seemed as though the "fix" was in on everything.

Another new idea popped up on the radio: an hour-long "talk show." (The idea was so radical, we put the words in quotes on our broadcast logs.) The show—with arguing and everything—was hosted by an ex-Marine named Joe Pyne, broadcasting from California. Just think—talk! For a whole hour? And not play any records at all? Aww, c'mon now. You gotta be kidding.

And the DJs were serving up zingers like, "Here's Ella Fitzgerald singing songs of her native Ireland" and "Here's the pickpocket song, 'I've Got You under My Coat'" and "Here's the chiropractor song, 'I Get a Kink Out of You.'"

It was some kind of decade, all right. I guess you really had to be there.

With the DJs and Bill Haley and the Comets and Elvis and rock and roll, a whole new group of ideas and techniques in the entertainment business began to appear.

Suddenly, kid performers, with what were termed "modest talents," were being exploited incredibly by producers, hustlers, promoters, bookers, and managers.

All of the above ingredients, mixed together, were leading us toward the music-biz scam.

It was truly an unbelievably simple scam.

Supposedly, promoters, bookers, and record guys would secretly *pay* the DJs to play their particular records on the airwaves. This way, certain records would thus be fed intravenously to the millions of twelve-to-fifteen-year-old listeners who would buy the records, which would then climb "the charts" (record sales figures published each week in the music-biz press). The records would then be played even more on the "chart-buster stations," which would sell even more records, and so on, ad nauseum. Man, we were having a ball.

They called it payola.

Now, payola was a great 1950s buzzword (although we hadn't invented the word "buzzword" yet). It fit the decade like a glove.

Florida was gradually to catch up with the rest of the nation. She seemed to begin to do so when all the major DJs, record producers and promoters, bookers, and many of the new kid stars, along with their managers and groupies, all met in Miami Beach for the first (and probably only) Annual DJ Convention. Once the word got around, a lot of station managers, program directors, and even record librarians came along to get in the act. During the event, many of the on-stage one-liners, gags, songs, parodies, and special material included heavily veiled references to the magic of the money—payola.

Near the end of the decade, the kingpin of all the DJs, television's handsome, boyish Dick Clark, had parlayed his "American Bandstand" TV program with its millions of kid viewers into becoming *the* powerhouse of creating instant new stars.

A couple major-market, "big name" DJs were found guilty of taking bribes and were banned from America's radio airwaves and the DJ biz. But Clark found that his show could almost make or break a new performer at will.

With his show reportedly earning some half-million bucks a year, Clark eventually became the subject of a Congressional investigation. The probe cleared the star of any bribe-taking. Investigators indicated, however, that his ownership of a record-pressing plant, a music-publishing company, and a talent-management firm probably had not hampered his show's success too badly.

As a matter of fact, it all seems kind of serene now, the payola, the rigged TV quiz shows, and all.

Just wait 'til we take a look at the *new* music biz lurking just ahead. What the kids are going to see and hear won't be over the airwaves as it is in the current music business.

It'll be on the computer screen.

And its style, content, intensity, and quality may well be totally controlled by a handful of producers who will have at their fingertips opportunities undreamed-of heretofore, for the grandest of all showbiz scams . . . of all time. All the payola dollars, all the under-the-table payoffs, kickbacks, skims, and scams combined will be but a tiny flyspeck compared to what the wondrous world of tomorrow's computers will produce.

Watch this.

First came records. (Phonograph records, they were called.) Then came radio stations and the disk jockeys who played those records over the air for folks to hear and enjoy. Folks then went out and sometimes bought some records. Simple enough so far.

Then the record producers decided to eliminate the element of chance and try to make sure that specific records were played over and over again. In Cleveland, known as a great "chart-bustin' town," one station would "break" a new release they had chosen by playing it eight to ten to fifteen times in a single day. Another station played a new record over and over twenty-eight times.

The brand-new, unknown record would become an instant local hit and would immediately begin to creep onto the national best-selling charts in the music-biz trade papers. You can see how all this begins to jell into a smoothly-functioning food chain, can't you? It works.

Then came TV, and the producers of contemporary sounds began to fill specific channels with their product being played over and over again, twenty-four hours a day. Kids could *watch* music as well as listen to it.

Now how about if you could actually connect the music directly to the Internet, and sort of put it on every computer screen in a given town? How about *that* for an idea?

Homes (and kids) all over will be hooked up to the Internet, and will be instantly reachable via their four-color, audio-producing computer screens. That big old TV set over in the corner of the room may go the way of those old phonograph records we told you about.

Next question: what—or who—is going to be overseeing and deciding the content of the programs? Or is anybody?

But first, let's say that these kids in those homes could actually punch up what they wanted to see, whatever group, performing whatever sounds they were to choose, whenever they wanted to. And suppose they were willing to pay, say, twenty-five cents to watch this special number. Or maybe even fifty cents, or even a buck for that matter. It's the same thing as those 900-number scams back a few chapters. You pay so much per minute for whatever you want.

Of course, remember, you're choosing that tune from a prepared list of, say, one hundred new releases. Hey! It's just like the old DJs on the radio! But now you get to *watch* it, too.

And instead of the promoters paying the DJs to play their tunes, *you* get to pay the computer people for having the computer play *your* choice (from *their* list).

Ah, you're way ahead of me—that rapid eye movement's giving you away again.

So how does the performance get on the playlist in the first place? you query.

Well, maybe there's a committee of some kind, you know, community leaders and all that, and they have a big meeting each week, and screen all the very best videos to come out that week in the whole country, and then carefully decide which ones are going to go on the hit list for that special week.

And then, maybe whichever ones get the most play from the kids each week get to stay on the list for the *next* week, or something like that. That's probably the way it will all work.

Suuure it will.

Or maybe the video producers decide to *pay* the computer company to put their new releases on the menu, you know, maybe so much per town for as many cities as they want to buy.

Or maybe once they get on the playlist, the producers have their own people out in Bugtussle call in and call in and call in to have their tune played over and over again.

Now remember, everybody in the loop is going to get to watch and listen to this little gem every time it's played. Only thing is, *everybody* is going to get to *pay* to have it played on their little screen.

Everything fine so far? Sure. No sweat.

Or how about this? How about if the computer company itself gets into the music biz and starts producing its *own* videos? *Now* whose videos do you think they're going to put on their hit list for the kids to choose from? Awww, come on, now. Hey, you can go start up your own network.

Now, let's say the computer company devises technology where the kids in Bugtussle can order up one tune, and the kids in Ottumwa can order up another. Sure. No problem. The technology is all here and it's all do-able as you read these lines.

It's only awaiting the millions of dollars required to set it all up. From there, it's but a few short steps to an entirely controlled musical culture being spoon-fed via computer screen to millions of kids who are paying for it on Daddy's phone bill. And it's all totally controlled by a single handful of companies, which will be reaping billions of dollars in sales revenues.

And so it's not too difficult to imagine, looking ahead into our scam world of the next century, a hundred million homes, all wired to computers with little kids staring at the rock groups on the screens. The kids are putting their nickels (dollars) in the jukebox via their phone bills so that they can watch a steady diet of totally controlled sounds. Brave new world, here we come.

The sounds are coming from a handful of production companies spoon-feeding their own fodder into the trough for the kids to slop up. (Overly graphic? Perhaps. But probably correct.)

And we'll see the kids—exactly as in the 1950s—mimicking the dress, stance, walk, language, facial expressions, attitudes—in short, the entire culture of whatever and whoever they see on that little screen, as our mercantile community races to produce whatever the kids will buy. (In the early 1960s, some thirty-seven thousand Beatles wigs were said to have sold out of New York stores in seventy-two hours.)

The next step, of course, just as in the rock revolution of 1955 to 1975, is products interwoven into the performers' acts. Whether it's their clothing—maybe a single white glove, T-shirts, black leather jackets, (did you think the black leather jacket people in 1956 just had a big meeting and decided to put on a huge advertising campaign—and it caught on?) shoes, shirts, earrings, nose-rings—or whatever you can think up, it will be on that little screen. Count on it. And chances are . . . we'll yearn for some good, old-fashioned payola.

29

We Have Met the Enemy—and They Are Us

AND SO I'VE TAKEN YOU on a grand tour of just a few thousand (approximately) of the more popular scams. We've met some of the perennial favorites that seem to be requested over and over again by you folks out there in Scam Land. And we've encountered some of the new ones that seem to really grab folks.

We've run the course, beginning with the historic railroad land-grab. We've cruised by the imported Bugattis of old Prince Michael of Austria and then over to "Dicky" Bolles and his famous disappearing land auction. We've moseyed through Fred Schulte's ostrich egg farm and Popham's Oyster Empire. We've even tiptoed into the careening world of cyberspace.

We've gazed in wonderment at the burgeoning development of a truly gigantic selling machine, a machine interconnecting millions upon millions of computer screens all over the planet under one gargantuan walnut shell. A selling machine all glued together by billions of miles of phone lines, cable, satellite uplinks and downlinks, fiber optics . . . and words we haven't even heard spoken yet.

A selling machine such as this one (it's bound to be here soon) will probably move more goods in just one season than all of our gross national product put together since

Bell tried to sell that silly telephone idea to Mark Twain.

Our generation will have been midwife to the birth of a whole new world of wonders.

We will watch folks being sold just about everything under the sun on their computer: classes in mud sculpture, skin creams, home-maintenance systems, security alarms, games, products, gimmicks, gadgets . . . and thousands of *investment opportunities!* (That's the best one.)

We'll see folks being sold shares in oil and gas wells where none exist; they'll be happily investing in limited partnerships although they won't know what they are.

We'll see them being sold shares in a paper corporation with no real assets. Tomorrow's giant selling machine will sell folks gold-mine stock, silver shares, offshore drilling contracts . . . everything from time-share units to transmission repair.

We'll see folks earning fantastic, unreal "returns" on their investments, which may be paid out of proceeds from sales made to other customers.

We'll see folks finding ever more exciting ways to learn the thrill of warm cider trickling down their earlobe while they peruse Grandaddy's Rules. The rules are always there for folks to rely on, if they'll just take advantage of them.

Tomorrow's con men will be developing new and inventive scams which will dwarf everything we've seen up to this point.

The principal target will probably remain the senior guys and gals. These are the folks who have some time to spare and are perhaps good listeners. Surveys repeatedly warn that the principal targets for scammers are the seniors, especially those who live alone.

We'll see our 1990s "channel-surfers" move into the museum alongside the old Atwater-Kent radio set with the big morning-glory horn loudspeakers, the Victrola record-changers with the dog listening to his master's voice, and the DuMont tv sets. (Did you know that we used to call them tv sets, with small letters, before we gave TV upper case—and maybe the upper hand?)

Now if some of this seems even a little bit farfetched to you, and if you *really* want to experience the passing of your generation into the impending computer/Internet world, just stop in at one of your neighborhood ultra-modern glitz-electronics stores. Stand in front of a seventy-foot-long wall of CDs, CD-ROMS, cassettes, cellular phones, tape decks, reel-to-reels, voice-and-music-audio-capability-full-color computers, laser readers, scanners, tuners, modems, bubble-jet printers . . . and ask to see—are you ready?—a *record player.*

It can be a quite moving and memorable experience, just from the blank stares on the clerks' faces alone.

The Senior Store Manager will say, as he did to me, with a meaningful, authoritative, and demonstrative series of loud, vertical handclaps, "Oh, you mean one of those things where the records used to fall right down on top of each other. Yeah, I remember. My folks had one of those. We don't carry 'em."

And we will probably see an entirely new culture arise. A culture of controlled music, art, drama, entertainment, and programming coming right out of our little computer screens. (Which, by the way, will quickly grow into wall-sized screens.) The "entertainment" will be produced, and owned, by that handful of music production companies I told you about, the ones which also own the computer network, Internet site, or cable system you're watching.

And if any of the above gives you mild concern, just think about how each new development will affect the existing businesses that provide those services today. Wonder how the current record companies will cope with computer-produced music. How about the small, independent record-pressing plants, attempting to produce quality music, but unable to get it played in the new media?

A whole new generation of Internet-surfers will have

replaced our friendly old channel-surfers. Folks in bed may no longer have to argue about who gets the clicker.

It has been suggested that the coming generations will face "information overload." Our grandkids will be provided so many products, services, games . . . so much material from which to choose that just making the choice could become a neurosis of the future.

The important point here is that with such an overload, the concealment of scams, from the very simplest to the grandest and most complex, will become an ever-more-simple maneuver for the master con artist to handle.

The challenge will be—as always—up to the individual. It'll be for the little guy and gal to learn, listen, and use common sense and street smarts when approached, either in person, over the phone, or in the little ten-inch computer screen.

And if you're a little short on common sense and street smarts, use Grandaddy's Rules. That's what they're for.

Because of its potential, the computer screen will probably prove to be your most vulnerable area. As one old-timer put it, "I don't want to have anything to do with a machine that's smarter than I am."

(Of course we know that there is a little human being in there someplace. No machine could be smart enough to do all those things by itself.)

And with the advent of the new age of scam in our brave new world, that little human being in there—along with his cohorts on the outside—is probably going to be the one who is out to separate you from some of your worldly goods.

It all goes back to a very simple, Old-World premise.

The premise was recently unearthed and brought back to the surface by Russell Baker in one of his columns in *The New York Times*. Baker was writing about radio's truly legendary comedic genius, iconoclast Fred Allen, who said that a certain network VP, when he came to work each morning at nine, found a molehill on his desk. His job was to make a mountain out of it by five o'clock.

Russell recalled a classic bit of Allen prose revered by Fred-Allen-ophiles everywhere (including this one). It occurred in the Allen radio program feature called "Allen's Alley."

During the feature, Fred conducted a sort of man-on-the-street public-opinion survey. He would visit with Mrs. Nussbaum (Minerva Pious), Falstaff Openshaw (Alan Reed, a later generation's Fred Flintstone), and a crusty old New England neighbor, Titus Moody, created by Parker Fennelly.

During one of the "Alley" features, Allen asked Titus Moody what he thought about radio.

Moody, in his thick, down-easter, "a-yup" brogue, replied, "Don't hold with furniture that talks."

Titus would have loved Grandaddy's Rules.

Appendix: Grandaddy's Rules: A Backward Glance

Some ways back, I sort of promised I'd assemble a whole bunch of Grandaddy's Rules for you in one neat pile, so you could peruse them at your leisure. Well, I guess that time has come.

Now both grandaddies were very real fellows, and their Rules were very real guidelines for their everyday activities. The Rules were usually handed down directly by both grandaddies from time to time, usually at giant family reunions.

Sometimes, the Rules would come secondhand to us kids as we were growing up. But we knew they were the real thing, whether or not they came directly. It seemed Daddy and Mother were forever using some quote or another, saying things like, "Well, like your grandaddy always said, blah, blah, blah."

And if we missed them from Mother and Daddy, there was always Uncle Milton, Aunt Margie, Uncle Alton, Aunt Georgia, Uncle Lamarr, Uncle Marion, Uncle Frank, Aunt Ethel and Uncle Crosson, Aunt Marie and Uncle Drane, Aunt Bernice and Uncle Smitty, Aunt Louise, Aunt Eunice, Aunt Ruby, and a whole peck of others. (When your mother and daddy had sixteen brothers and sisters between them, all in Florida, and when each grandaddy had about eleven apiece of their own, also all in Florida, you end up with about a hundred or so kinfolk in just those two generations at any given family reunion.)

I'll locate the rules by chapter for you, and maybe add a couple of comments.

Rule #1: There almost ain't never nuthin' fer nuthin'; INTRODUCTION.

It's perhaps ungrammatical, but very much to the point. This rule encompasses every deal done, every transaction consummated, every handshake shook in any bin-ness deal.

Rule #2: You learn sump'n new every day . . . unless you're very, very careful; CHAPTER ONE.

This one was sort of like that Instant Teaching Machine sign that Hank Thompson hung on that malfunctioning soda pop dispenser I told you about. Papa Knight used this rule all through his Florida legislature days.

Rule #3: Nobody ever pulled no rabbit out of no hat without carefully puttin' one in there first; CHAPTER ONE.

This rule was espoused by both grandaddies, especially Papa Johnson when he was talking about the wild and crazy land boom in the 1920s. It was also one of Papa Knight's favorite mottoes when talking about some of his moves in the legislature around 1900.

Rule #4: If they's talkin' to you about pie in the sky, chances are they's gonna make it with your dough; CHAPTER THREE.

This one applied to virtually everything that took place in Florida during the land boom from 1918 to 1928. Many natives felt that the great hue and cry of the sales hustlers then was just that: a lot of pie in the sky, and they knew *they* were going to have to come up with the dough.

Rule #5: Preacher Robinson's Credo: I wanna be around when the meek inherit the earth, so I can watch the *un-meek* take it away from 'em; CHAPTER FIVE.

Preacher Robinson really did used to say this. It was one

of his favorite sayings at the big church suppers out at the beach. Late in his career, Papa Johnson simply scooped it up and claimed it for his own. He would use it for just about any occasion, whether it fit or not.

Rule #6: If it seems too good to be true, chances are, it is; CHAPTER SIX.

This one will apply to almost any scam being pulled on just about anybody.

Rule #7: Man will not eat his own kind. He will, hy-ever, skin 'em; CHAPTER EIGHT.

This is the ancient, anthropological rule, adapted to modern (1919) times in Florida.

Rule #8: The large print giveth and the small print taketh away; CHAPTER NINE.

The old cracker farmers, bin-ness men, and politicians always knew when fellows could be counted on to stand by their word, whether it was written on a piece of paper or not. However, by the turn of the century, farmers and backwoodsmen began to learn that they had better get it in writing and get someone to *read* that writing for them, unless they knew the other fellow real well. (Or unless he was kinfolk.)

Rule #9: Experience is what helps you recognize your mistakes—when you make them again; CHAPTER TEN.

Papa Johnson, as he started over again in St. Pete, would have remembered this one real well . . . and it will stand us in good stead today.

Rule #9-b: Either do it better, or faster, or longer than the next feller, and you'll always make out all right; CHAPTER TWENTY-THREE.

Papa Johnson's rule for being a good salesman.

Rule #10: If you're gonna go wrong, go slow. You won't have to back up far to clean up your mess; CHAPTER FIFTEEN.

Of course, the real trick is knowing when you're going wrong!

Rule #11: Friend, if you'll buy that, I've got some land in the Everglades I want to talk to you about; CHAPTER FOURTEEN.

This became a classic rejoinder by both grandaddies in response to just about any deal they encountered.

Rule #13-a: Don't never go into bin-ness with a fella named Skip; CHAPTER EIGHTEEN.

This good old rule really came into its own during the flower of the land boom, when companies were created and dissolved overnight, so very few guys wanted to be called by the nickname of "Skip." It just wasn't good bin-ness.

Rule #14: The Old-Fashioned Cracker Payment Plan: Everything down and nothing a month for the rest of your life; CHAPTER FOURTEEN.

This oldie-but-goodie goes right along with one of the grandaddies' other sayings, "If you can't pay as you go, maybe you're goin' too fast." These applied very well during the Panic of (pick a year, any year at all. They had one almost every season when the Northern folks went home and they had to close the stores).

Rule #15: You always do bin-ness with your kinfolk; CHAPTER FIFTEEN.

In every tiny hamlet, village, and town in the Old South, bin-ness transactions could be observed taking place for but one reason: "He's family. His momma and my grandaddy were cousins." Even when a new salesman (this one) pointed out that the competing salesman's product wasn't doing the customer any good, the answer was, "Heck, I know that. But he takes good care of us, and his momma was my daddy's first sweetheart. (That's not even kinfolk, but it's close enough.) And that would be all that was necessary. It's a good way to make sure you don't get skinned by any smooth-talking strangers. (You just might get skinned by someone you know!)

The un-numbered rules:

There is no danger in running into debt. It's running into your *creditors* that gives you problems; CHAPTER ONE.

If there exists a way to get around it, somebody, somewhere will find a way to get around it; CHAPTER ONE.

For every plus, somewhere there's a minus; CHAPTER TWO.

For every gain, somewhere there's a loss; CHAPTER TWO.

Rail Rule: If the rails don't come to your town, mister, you don't have a town; CHAPTER TWENTY.

You never really know just how much you can do . . . until you try to undo some of what you've done; CHAPTER TWENTY-TWO.

So there you have a quick tour of Grandaddy's Rules. It's not all of them, but it's enough for a starter.

Keep them handy, because someday, somewhere, some smooth-talking jasper is going to sidle up to you, or some cutie is going to pop up on that magic little Internet screen just a'smiling at you. And they're going to be pitching a deal that's just absolutely too con-sarned, dog-boned good to resist.

And *that's* when you're going to be so glad that you've got your list of Grandaddy's Rules handy. Just flip her open to whatever page . . . use any rule you like, whatever one comes up first.

Because the best rule of all is that the rules are interchangeable.

Good luck out there in Scam Land!

Bibliography

Books

Dodrill, David. *Selling the Dream; the Gulf American Corporation and the Building of Cape Coral, Florida.* Tuscaloosa: University of Alabama Press, 1993.

Eichenwald, Kurt. *Serpent on the Rock.* New York City: HarperBusiness, division of HarperCollins Publishers, 1995.

McIver, Stuart. *Glimpses of South Florida History.* Miami: Florida Flair Books, 1988.

————-. *Rascals, and Scalawags.* Miami: Florida Flair Books, 1995.

Rogers, William Warren. *Outposts on the Gulf.* Tallahassee: Florida State University Press, 1987.

Schulte, Fred. *Fleeced.* New York: Prometheus Books, 1995.

Tebeau, Charlton. *A History of Florida.* Coral Gables: University of Miami Press, 1980.

Tuckwood, Jan, and Kleinberg, Elliot. *Pioneers in Paradise.* Marietta: Longstreet Press, 1994.

Newspapers, Periodicals, Services, and Programs

Gold Coast Magazine (1975-1990), McCormick, Bernard, ed.

The News: Knight-Ridder newspaper serving South Palm Beach County.

The New York Times and *The New York Times* News Service: for several stories on Florida, Boca Raton, and Florida scams.

Palm Beach Post: Cox Newspapers' multi-generational publication for all the Palm Beaches.

Research in Review, Stephenson, Frank, ed.

St. Petersburg Times: the Poynter family's legendary newspaper for nearly a century; source of stories on Treasure Island and on legendary mayor Noel Mitchell.

"60 Minutes": various segments.

South Florida History Magazine (Summer and Fall 1994), McIver, Stuart, and Brown, Natalie, eds.

Sun-Sentinel Newspapers: Gore Newspapers from Fort Lauderdale into South Palm Beach County.

The Tampa Tribune: outstanding Tampa Bay and Tampa publication.

The Washington Post: especially Albert Crenshaw's article on the repeat pattern of senior victims of scams.